FROM PRISON TO PEACE:

THE PRODIGAL DAUGHTER

MARY A. FAHER

WESTBOW
PRESS®
A DIVISION OF THOMAS NELSON
& ZONDERVAN

WestBow Press books may be ordered through booksellers or by contacting:

WestBow Press
A Division of Thomas Nelson & Zondervan
1663 Liberty Drive
Bloomington, IN 47403
www.westbowpress.com
1 (866) 928-1240

ISBN: 978-1-9736-6451-2 (sc)
ISBN: 978-1-9736-6450-5 (e)

Print information available on the last page.

WestBow Press rev. date: 11/06/2019

**God cannot give us a Happiness
and Peace apart from Himself,
because it is not there.
- C.S. Lewis**

Thanksgiving to the LORD for His Great Works of Deliverance!

Oh, give thanks to the LORD, for He is good! For His mercy endures forever. Let the redeemed of the LORD say so, Whom He has redeemed from the hand of the enemy, And gathered out of the lands, From the east and from the west, From the north and from the south. They wandered in the wilderness in a desolate way; They found no city to dwell in. Hungry and thirsty, Their soul fainted in them. Then they cried out to the LORD in their trouble, And He delivered them out of their distresses.

And He led them forth by the right way, That they might go to a city for a dwelling place. Oh, that men would give thanks to the LORD for His goodness, And for His wonderful works to the children of men.

For He satisfies the longing soul, And fills the hungry soul with goodness. Those who sat in darkness and in the shadow of death, Bound in affliction and irons—Because they rebelled against the words of God, And despised the counsel of the Most High, Therefore He brought down their heart with labor; They fell down, and there was none to help.

Then they cried out to the LORD in their trouble, And He saved them out of their distresses. He brought them out of darkness and the shadow of death, And broke their chains in pieces. Oh, that men would give thanks to the LORD for His goodness, And for His wonderful works to the children of men! For He has broken the gates of bronze, And cut the bars of iron in two.

Fools, because of their transgression, And because of their iniquities, were afflicted. Their soul abhorred all manner of food, And they drew near to the gates of death.

Then they cried out to the LORD in their trouble, And He saved them out of their distresses. He sent His word and healed them, And delivered them from their destructions. Oh, that men would give thanks to the LORD for His goodness, And for His wonderful works to the children of men! Let them sacrifice the sacrifices of thanksgiving, And declare His works with rejoicing.

Those who go down to the sea in ships, Who do business on great waters, They see the works of the LORD, And His wonders in the deep. For He commands and raises the stormy wind, Which lifts up the waves of the sea. They mount up to the heavens, They go down again to the depths; Their soul melts because of trouble.

They reel to and fro, and stagger like a drunken man, And are at their wits' end. Then they cry out to the LORD in their trouble, And He brings them out of their distresses. He calms the storm, So that its waves are still.

Then they are glad because they are quiet; So He guides them to their desired haven. Oh, that men would give thanks to the LORD for His goodness, And for His wonderful works to the children of men! Let them exalt Him also in the assembly of the people, And praise Him in the company of the elders.

He turns rivers into a wilderness, And the watersprings into dry ground; A fruitful land into barrenness, For the wickedness of those who dwell in it.

He turns a wilderness into pools of water, And dry land into watersprings. There He makes the hungry dwell, That they may establish a city for a dwelling place, And sow fields and plant vineyards, That they may yield a fruitful harvest.

He also blesses them, and they multiply greatly; And He does not let their cattle decrease. When they are diminished and brought low Through oppression, affliction, and sorrow,

He pours contempt on princes, And causes them to wander in the wilderness where there is no way; Yet He sets the poor on high, far from affliction, And makes their families like a flock.

The righteous see it and rejoice, And all iniquity stops it's mouth. Whoever is wise will observe these things, And they will understand the lovingkindness of the LORD.

- Psalm 107

ACKNOWLEDGEMENTS

I am humbled and grateful for all that I have gone through and how God has chosen me for the awesome task of spreading the good news. Jesus Lives, Jesus Saves, Jesus is the Way! I have learned to live in the moment, day by day and if anxiety or fear find their way to my door, all I need to say is: "God, I love You and I need you, come into my heart please."

I have learned step by step how to live my life God focused, from God Himself, through His word, the Bible and that I am loved, me, Mary A. Faher, felon along with a whole list of sins. I have to admit that my biggest sin was pride. I thought that I was smart enough and capable of leading my own life…thank you very much. I admit to being strong willed and while I loved God, I didn't think I needed Jesus to be the go between for my prayers to God. I had learned in Sunday school that Jesus was love, but somewhere along the journey I became self-centered, not Christ-centered.

I realize now that God had been trying to get my attention for a long time and I was too busy doing "ME" that I didn't hear Him or maybe on some level I didn't want to hear Him. I have been blessed beyond, God has shown me His Mercy and Grace. I want to thank each of you for your patience, prayers, and your faith in me, not to give up, there was a purpose for going to prison, I am so grateful for each and every one of you:

To my Son and his wife, Ian and Elizabeth for being patient with me when I couldn't understand something, for always being available when I needed them. And of course, the huge task of liquidating everything I owned.

My step-father, James Stephens who never gave up on me and continued to visit me and feed me candy and pop. I began to call him, my sugar daddy. God blessed us in that we were able to find each other and love each other.

My best friend, Jan Johnson, that always encouraged me, loved me and accepted me just the way I am. My life would not be complete without her.

My friend, Jennifer Glazer that never stopped sending me uplifting pictures and cards. Keeping me focused on when I would be free.

My friend, Ingrid Doerksen, who sent me the entire series, The Outlander, which made the days go by faster, but most importantly I began to see that men could be gentlemen and trustworthy, at least in fiction. In addition to all that, the magazine Happiness was enjoyed by not only me, but other inmates as well.

My animal lover, Kathryn Bury for taking in my dog Buddha. I am so grateful to her for opening up her home to him and loving him like he was her own.

My Grateful Dead buddy, Bruce Blaha who took of my cats, Tia and Lil Bob, literally saving them from the pound.

My prayer friend, Brenda Davis for her amusing letters and the prayer group she was in, praying for me.

It really has taken a village to keep me focused and taking each day one by one. The light of my family and friends, helped to keep the darkness at bay. I am so blessed…

To Moms in Prayer for giving me the <u>Henry Morris Study Bible</u> that was the key to opening the door for the intimate relationship I now have with God living in peace and joy.

And all of the members of my support group, THE CEMENT BENCH, on Facebook, for keeping it going in my absence with membership up to over 11,000 when I finally was released. And to all others who have prayed and sent blessings.

And to:

Those that follow Jesus' LIGHT and those that don't, afraid to either start or begin anew. Those that have lost Hope.

All of those who are seeking an intimate relationship with God, who desire to know what it is to be truly alive, living in peace and joy.

DEDICATION

I dedicate this book to Mrs. Dorothy Knowlton, my early Sunday School teacher, who taught me that I might be the only Bible someone would ever read, whose kindness and compassion will be with me forever.

Living Before the World

Beloved, I beg you as sojourners and pilgrims, abstain from fleshly lusts which war against the soul, having your conduct honorable among the Gentiles, that when they speak against you as evildoers, they may, by your good works which they observe, glorify God in the day of visitation.
- 1 Peter 2:11-12 NKJV

You show that you are a letter from Christ, the result of our ministry, written not with ink but with the Spirit of the living God, not on tablets of stone but on tablets of human hearts.
- 2 Corinthians 3:1-11 NKJV

For you are all sons of God through faith in Christ Jesus. For as many of you were baptized into Christ have put on Christ.
- Galatians 3:26-27

This true story is important, it's the journey of a prisoner, a slave to sin, coming to God and accepting His Son, Jesus Christ as her Lord, Redeemer and Savior. He was the sinless lamb sacrificed for us so that our sins would be washed away by His blood.

It is a story that other believers can understand, live for and be strengthened. This book is about sharing His amazing love with others. I, as the author, am not important. Before my redemption, I would have never been able to make that statement. Pride would have blinded me from the truth and arrogance would have poisoned this entire book, and it is that arrogance that poisons our futures. In John 3:30, John the Baptist said, "He must become greater; we must become lesser."

Make no mistake, all Glory is to be given to God the Father who is waiting…waiting for all of us to be united.

Dear Heavenly Father, help me to become Your humble servant so that I might see You and understand you more fully. Lord help me to live with You as my top priority in my life. Lord I ask, let it be about you and not about me. In Jesus' name … Amen

No discipline seems pleasant at the time, but painful. Later on, however, it produces a harvest of righteousness and peace for those who have been trained by it.
- Hebrews 12:11

Contents

INTRODUCTION

Life is not about the destination, it is about the journey. We have all heard this, but what does it mean? Each journey is as different as there are people on the planet. I like to think that mine is unique, however, I have been humbled enough to understand that each of us are born and we die and there are many similarities in between that we share. In writing this book, I wanted to share my experience so that someone who can relate can understand that nothing in life can happen to you that you can't still go on to live the best part of your life. In my case, after the darkness, I am now living the best of my life, living my greatest desire which is to have an intimate and loving relationship with our Father, our Lord Jesus Christ.

From the beginning of my journey, in incarceration, I felt God's presence and a hunger to know His word and find peace and joy that only He could give me. I had no idea of the many blessings that I would receive, it was beyond any expectations that I could have had.

I started writing this book shortly after my arrival at the Huron Valley Correctional Facility, Ypsilanti, Michigan. I was broken, anxious, angry, at times disoriented and on the verge of giving up all hope and death seeming to be the answer for ridding myself of the pain. I have always thought of myself as a strong woman and this woman was shattered.

I hope that you can see and feel the transition and redemption that I went through, resulting with this strong woman, even stronger, peaceful, more focused, and so grateful to have gone through this chapter of my life. Yes, I am grateful that I went to prison. It was a gift from our loving Father, God to get my attention and in doing so, gave me the desire of my heart, a life of intimacy with my first love, Jesus. I live a life of complete joy, peace, truth, light and love. God has blessed me, indeed.

CHAPTER 1

BEYOND THE BLINDING BARBED WIRE

For I have heard the slander of many: fear was on every side: while they took counsel together against me, they devised to take away my life.

But I trusted in thee, O Lord: I said, Thou art my God. My times are in thy hand: deliver me from the hand of mine enemies, and from them that persecute me. Make thy face to shine upon thy servant: save me for thy mercies sake.
– Psalm 31:13-14

O Lord my God, in you I put my trust; save me from all those who persecute me; and deliver me lest they tear me like a lion, rending me in pieces, while there is none to deliver.

O Lord my God, if I have done this: if there is iniquity in my hands, if I have repaid evil to him who was at peace with me, or have plundered my enemy without cause, let the enemy pursue

me and overtake me; yes, let him trample my life to the earth,
and lay my honor in the dust.
- Psalm 7:1-5 NKJV

Sitting in the back of a Berrien County Sheriff's Department SUV, with my eyes closed trying to block out what was happening to me. I was aware of the sun shining in between the clouds, just like in the movies, the sky is fast forwarding, bringing me closer to my destination, my "home" for the next 23 months to 10 years, all depending on my good behavior.

I was "riding out" with a woman from a community close to mine. She told me this wasn't her "first rodeo," that she was a (PV) parole violator, having caught a new case while she was still on parole. My mind was reeling trying to grasp the prison lingo. She was going on about what I should expect once we got there. I was trying to pay attention, but my racing mind wouldn't focus. My brain had been shutting down ever since I was sentenced and housed in the County jail until MDOC (Michigan Department of Corrections) was ready for me. After a while it just became noise and I tuned it out. I knew that she had meant well, but I hadn't asked for it and all I really wanted was silence. The two officers in the front seat, in front of the iron grid were quiet, speaking sporadicly and I could hear the murmur of the radio. There wasn't anything that anyone could have said to me that would have prepared me for what I was going to encounter.

As the ride brought me closer to my destination, my hands were becoming numb because the manacles were too tight. They were attached to a waist chain causing further restriction of movement, resulting in pain and stiffness. I just closed my eyes trying to block out the fear and the anger I felt, because of betrayal. Betrayed by the men, that I had worked for and believed and by the judicial system.

I felt the slowing down of the vehicle and heard the clicking of the turn signal, announcing that our arrival was coming sooner than I thought. It appeared that we were in a residential area with the houses sparsely spaced and then, there it was…the sign welcoming us to Women's Huron Valley Correctional Facility in Ypsilanti, MI. I had never been to Ypsilanti and God willing, would never be again after serving my sentence.

As we turned into the drive, the sun was shining brightly in the cloudless sky. I found myself squinting and the barbed wire and fence were shining like diamonds, like snow on a cold bright winter's morning. The fence was on both sides of the driveway and enveloped the entire compound. I felt sick to my stomach, like I needed to vomit. It wasn't the height or the length of the fence, it was the coiled barbed wire that was on top of the fence and also the coils at ground level lining the fence. It felt surreal to me as if I were part of a prison movie. This was REAL, this was my reality and there wasn't anything I could do about it. I felt so alone, abandoned and in the direct control of MDOC, their property and as such, theirs to control, direct, bend or break, at their will. My mother said there were going to be days like this, but I am sure she never imagined this for her daughter. One thing I was grateful for was the fact that she was not alive to see this, it would have broken her heart.

I have always been head strong and rebellious, and the rebel in me was telling myself "They can control my body, but they will never control my mind or soul." I had always taken pride in being a free spirit, doing it my way."

The SUV stopped in what looked like a gravel parking lot, on closer look, it had been paved at one time, however, there were holes and chunks of asphalt all around, giving it the appearance of a junk yard. It was obvious that maintaining the drive had not been a priority. I looked around and saw other vans were there before us, so we were going to have to wait our turn. I could feel my chest tighten, my breathing was becoming more rapid and I was really shutting down. When that happens my eyesight and hearing are affected. It is as if my body is shielding me from sensory overload. From somewhere I heard, "Just breathe, one step at a time and one day at a time." I knew it was God, my Lord, who I trusted above all others. I knew that He wouldn't forsake me.

The SUV's door slid open and the deputy motioned for me to get out. I must have had a blank stare on my face because she had to hasten me again to get out. That was much easier said than done. As I started to shift my weight so that I could move, I started to panic, my mobility had been deteriorating for quite some time, due to the stress that I had been under for the last two years, weight gain which in turn caused my arthritis to flare up and lack of activity had led to loss of strength. My neuropathy was continuing to deteriate and not being on my medications for the last ten days didn't help. With all that said, it was no wonder that I felt trapped and unable to move. It didn't help that I was in an awkward position and couldn't use my arms and hands for leverage. I was in the back seat with my fellow inmate behind me and no place to turn around.

The deputy again, motioned for me to get out, now! I finally found my voice and told her I was having trouble, was there any way that she can assist me in getting out? It was obvious that I was in distress, couldn't she see that? She slid the seat in front of me forward, making more room for me to maneuver. I was able to sit on the floor board, scoot to the opening, dangle my legs out of the opening, put my feet solidly on the ground and it took all the strength I had, I stood up and out, freeing up the space for the inmate to follow behind. How much easier it would have been if only the deputy would have helped me out.

The deputy led us to the gate where a Corrections Officer (C.O.) opened the locking mechanism, standing aside for us to be led by the deputy to the intake area of the prison. PRISON, this was PRISON. I still couldn't believe that I was there. It felt like a dream, the kind you struggle to wake up from.

My attorney certainly had not prepared me for the possibility of going to prison. He thought that I would get probation as recommended by the parole office, and at the worst, some jail time, but prison was only a slim possibility. Not only was I not prepared, neither were my family and friends so that we could have made plans for the "what if."

Intake is the process that each felon goes through, in essence, stripping away "the you" and replacing it with "the prisoner." I undressed, giving the county jump suit and sandals to the C.O. to give to the deputy to take back to the county. I had to throw away my personal underwear because I was going to be issued a whole new wardrobe.

After taking a shower and having a full body search, I was given the clothing that I was going to wear for the next 23 months. It included the "state blues" which were the official clothes to be worn on visits and to classes, etc. Because I was a new prisoner and not a P.V. I received new clothing as opposed to the used items that they were getting. So, I got the new and the inmate that came in with me, got the used. I was then led to the area where the photograph was taken that was going to be used on the state I.D. My hair was still wet and as I sat there, I asked if I was allowed to smile? All of the felon pictures I had seen at the post office and on the television looked so stern, crazy and scary. I was allowed to smile and I did. As I was tying my state issued shoes, the C.O. gave me my I.D. and it was the first time I saw my number, 939508. It was the number I will carry with me to death, along with the title of being a felon.

It was as if I was on auto-pilot, doing exactly what was requested and asking no questions. I was led to a holding cell, and yes, there was a cement bench, I had to smile at that. There were six other women already in the cell waiting for the next step in the intake process. What struck me as odd, was that most of the women had been there before. There were only a couple of us "newbies." That stunned me, in fact, later on I was to learn that 83% of the felon's return, either as a P.V. violating a stipulation of their parole or a P.V. with a new case. I made a vow to myself that I was going to do whatever it took to stay out of here.

As I sat on the cement bench, I had a few minutes to myself, to ponder just what had gone so terribly wrong. How could it be that I was back on yet another cement bench? I never dreamed that I would again sit on that hard, cold slab, let alone that it would be in prison.

One of the things I learned from the first cement bench was that nothing is by accident, there is a reason for all of it, keeping that in mind was a little comforting and I knew that God would see me through it. The saying "If God brought you to it, He will lead you through it," and I was counting on that. I knew that many people would say that I took a wrong turn on my journey, however, I knew that in time, I would come to understand what the purpose for this mess was. As with my entire life, the darkest times seemed to result in lessons that helped me grow and prepare me for the next step on the journey. So in actuality there are no wrong turns, but while you are in the dark it can be a terrifying time and this was where I was at. I would have plenty of time to work it out. I never was one to just go with the flow, only dead fish do that. I wondered how that was going to work for me now that MDOC owned me. Trying to breathe, I found comfort in knowing that God was with me and together, we would get through this. I decided there and then to do my time and not let time do me.

As I was being issued my clothing and bedding, which was to last a year before it could be changed out for new ones, it occurred to me that I have been paying state taxes for many years and that meant that I had paid for all of this, in an odd kind of way. I was issued:

- 3 pair of slacks/state blues
- 1 "all season" coat
- 5 pairs of socks
- 1 pair of thermal underwear
- 2 pair of pajamas
- 1 pair of winter gloves
- 2 pairs of shorts

- 3 blouses/state blues
- 1 pair of shoes
- 3 bras
- 9 panties
- 1 robe
- 1 winter stocking cap
- 1 package of Kotex

Along with:

- 1 duffel bag
- 2 wool blankets
- 3 towels
- 3 wash cloths

- 1 pillow
- 2 laundry bags
- 2 twin sheet sets
- 2 rolls of toilet paper

For the past few years, God has been whispering in my ear that too much "stuff," would only get in the way in our relationship and could in fact, the "stuff" could be an addiction. Materialism definitely is not of God, which only can mean that it is of Satan, the God of this world. So in my mind, I could only bring something into the house when something else was taken out, usually donated, making room for the new acquisition. I also intellectualized that I was upgrading, so "stuff" wasn't a problem for me. At some level I must have known that my thinking was a little askew, so I had asked God to help me with the process of letting go. I certainly didn't have this in mind! Apparently this was a lesson that I needed and there must not have been any other way to learn it or I just wasn't listening, which was probably the case.

I can tell you from the "stuff" I was issued, I was going to find out exactly how it was to be to have less, much less and not only that, but the quality I was used to was not going to be the same quality. I was going to learn the difference between need and want.

By this time my brain and body had almost completely shut down. The C.O. in charge of intake had me come and sit at her desk. She started asking me questions that on any other normal day would be easy to answer. As I sat there I was feeling more and more like an ignorant criminal, that I must belong here. I was agitated, anxious, tired, and becoming more and more like a zombie. I have to say that the C.O. was very understanding, obviously she had seen this before, so I wasn't the only ignorant criminal she had ever seen. That however, did not bring me any comfort or help the situation. A huge part of the problem was that I, like so many others had become dependent on technology. My cell phone had my son's phone number for emergencies, it also had my best friend's phone number. I just sat there with a blank mind and I am sure my expression matched my brain.

After she was done with me, she had me go back to the holding cell and call the next prisoner for their time of questioning. While we sat there, lunch was served by other prisoners who worked in the kitchen. I took the top off of the tray and was surprised! This meal wasn't what I was expecting, it was something altogether different.

While I was in the county jail, a couple of the women, who had been to prison before, told me the food in state prison was so much better than in county jail. This was definitely not the case, it must have been the cook's day off. The mashed potatoes were watery, without any salt or pepper, very bland…tasteless. The greens were slimy and I was clueless what the meat was, unidentifiable. The only good thing was the cake even without frosting.

Everyone was given a Styrofoam cup and told to keep it, that it would be the only cup we would be issued and that we could place an order for a plastic cup once we were set up for the store. I had no idea what store was or how to do it. We all quickly wrote our names on the cups with the mini pencils, like the ones at miniature golf. Again we were reminded to take care of the one cup we were going to be issued. I decided right there and then that I was going to guard my cup and pencil like they were my only valuables, which of course, they were to me.

We were given an assessment test to see where we scored in relation to any type of addictions, mental health issues and what we hoped to attain while we were incarcerated. I remember thinking to myself that I thought all I had to do was show up, do the time with good behavior and have early parole, which for me would be in 23 months. It was beginning to look like they were going to make me jump through hoops before I was ever going to be released.

I sat there, trying to get my brain to function, hoping that the sugar in the cake would be enough to jump start the neurons, which was difficult because I was so stunned to believe I was actually there! What did I intend to get out of prison? I intended to get out alive! To survive. It was at that point that my conversation with God started up and I made my desires known to Him. I remember saying, "Lord, when I leave this place, I want to be physically, mentally, and spiritually stronger than today. In fact, better than ever before." I didn't know exactly where I could write that on the form in the space provided, so I just wrote, lose weight.

That seemed like a reasonable enough goal, however, at 100 lbs. or more over my ideal weight, it would take more than will power, and it would take an act of God to achieve. I was suffering physically from the effects of morbid obesity, with arthritis in my knees, ankles and feet, and most of all, vascular neuropathy, making walking difficult and standing for any length of time was almost impossible. I had been diagnosed with Complex PTSD which added a whole array of other problems, the biggest being sleep deprived, forgetful and foggy.

I sat there waiting for everyone else to finish their needs assessment, tired, but not sleepy, having no focus at all. My hyper vigilance was in high gear, screaming **DANGER, DANGER, DANGER**, putting me on overload and sending me into near panic. I knew that the 24/7 adrenaline coursing through my body had taken a real toll on my body and my mind. As my Doctor had explained to me, over exposure to adrenaline becomes toxic, the body and brain weren't made to tolerate long term effects. I have had hypervigilance all of my life, manageable at times and for the last decade it had been in overdrive. I knew that imprisonment was not going to be easy on any level, however, knowing what I knew about PTSD, I was in for a long stay.

PTSD
(Post-Traumatic Stress Disorder)

Many survivors of trauma have an automatic nervous system that overstimulates the flight or fight response. This over stimulation means the adrenaline levels are chronically high, for extended periods of time which can have serious impacts on the body. Symptoms can include:

- difficulty in falling asleep or staying asleep
- feeling irritable or having outbursts of anger, memory and concentration problems
- hypervigilance (startling easily) and feeling that you have no reserve of energy to help you heal.

Some trauma survivors express the trauma through Immune related illnesses such as chronic fatigue, fibro-myalgia, irritable bowel syndrome, headaches and severe tension and anxiety. Left to itself, PTSD can lead to jumpiness as well as fear, terror and sometimes, suicide.

CHAPTER 2

MA'AM, YES MA'AM
MA'AM NO MA'AM

Let me not be ashamed, O Lord; for I have called thee: Let the wicked be ashamed, and let them be silent in the grave. Let the lying lips be put to silence; which speak grievous things proudly and contemptuously against the righteous.
- Psalm 31:17-18

It was time…time for those of us in the holding cell to be escorted to the unit that would house us until we had been medically and mentally cleared as well as being classified for security reasons and they would observe how well we obeyed orders and rules. Unit 9, RGC, houses all levels of prisoners. Murderers, sexual predators, junkies, drug dealers, thieves, DUI's and more for approximately 30-45 days before being moved to the grounds where the general population resided. Because everyone was housed there and there are extra security measures taken and I was told it would be the worst part of my prison term…so that if I could survive that, I could survive anything. In fact, the next 3-5 days were going to be absolutely the worst due to our being quarantined to make sure we were not bringing in any disease, such as TB or any other communicable disease. We would have a cell to ourselves and would be only let out to use the bathroom and shower, to limit other prisoner and staff exposure to us. I was trying to mentally prepare myself and knew that God would be with me.

We all lined up against the wall with our duffle bags. I watched as the women in front of me picked up their bag and as I began to lift mine, it didn't budge. My muscle strength was poor at best, so trying not to panic, I just dragged mine behind me and that was still hard to do. The intake area is actually attached to Unit 9, so we didn't have very far to walk. I knew I could do solitary confinement, maybe I could relax a little, knowing that I would be safe in my cell. As a matter of fact, I had been living as a hermit for over a year, rarely going out. To add to that, I am an only child, so I am used to being by myself. I was so thankful that at an early age, God told me I would never be alone, so in reality, I wasn't going to be alone here either.

I was raised in an abusive home and at times I needed a refuge when my body and spirit was bruised and broken. God had always been a way of life for me and I was going to need Him and I had already let Him know it. It has always been during the darkest times of my life that He felt the nearest to me. His presence would sustain me, I would get through this! I could feel Him with me now.

I first experienced God when I was about 11 years old, and this is what I remember about that experience:

> **I knew that God was LOVE always, in all ways! It was Easter time and they always showed movies about Jesus. I think it was the King of Kings, with Jeffery Hunter playing Jesus. I had watched the movie and I was in a real emotional state. I was shaken to the core, seeing Jesus abused, scourged and nailed to that cross to die.**
>
> **My mother had let me sleep upstairs in the double bed, with real springs! It was a treat, in all reality; I was out of her hair! I was tossing and turning… How could they have killed our Lord who was so good and only wanted to help people? He was LOVED by so many! How could they not believe He was the Son of God! Oh, how He suffered. Who was I, just a little girl in Benton Harbor, Michigan…I didn't have anyone LOVING me, what was going to happen to me, I was so alone? I cried long and hard, the kind that gives you a headache. I remember seeing a blue light in the room, I remember feeling calmness and I remember hearing: "I will always LOVE you and be with you, you will never be alone!"**

Now I can't say I heard that with my ears, but some way, somehow, I heard it. I was instantly in a place of PEACE. At that time, I interpreted it as God and I still BELIEVE that to this day.

Nothing the P.V.'s had talked about to prepare me would come close to the reality that I was about to endure. The prison was severely over- crowded and the wing of the building that was normally used for the "Quarantines" was full. As we stood at the front desk, the officer told each of us where we were going to bunk. Of course it meant nothing to me, but the women who had been here before gasped at the news and I took it to mean that it wasn't very good news. We were going to be housed in the wing for Special Alternative Incarceration (S.A.I.) or better known as Boot Camp. It really was a good thing that at that time, I hadn't a clue what any of it meant.

After dragging my duffel back to my cell, the C.O., whom later I was to learn was a Corporal, screeched for us to line up in the hallway, behind the yellow line, NOW! I was exhausted, it had been a long day and all I wanted to do was to flop down on the bunk and not move, giving my body and brain a rest, like the black screen on a computer. Now, that wasn't going to happen! My body ached, it was stiff and I was having difficulty walking, let alone standing. All of the symptoms I was experiencing were possibly due to the fact that I had not received my daily medication which included an anti-inflammation pill for my osteo-arthritis, medication for my neuropathy, along with my daily dosages of thyroid medication, for the last 10 days! Jails and prisons do not set medications as a high priority, so I had no idea when I would finally get relief.

Two Corporals stood at attention in front of us, ram rod stiff, glaring at us, seeming not to blink. I felt that "punch in the gut" feeling and could feel the blood drain from my face. I kept telling myself over and over again…stay alert! The taller of the two Corporals stepped forward and yelled, "While you are housed on this wing, you will NOT, I repeat, NOT look at the trainees, you will NOT engage with the trainees in any way. Do you understand?" I nodded and a few of the women answered yes. "I didn't hear you!" she yelled. Instinctly, I took my cue from a couple of the women in our group and yelled "Yes Ma'am." It was getting harder by the minute to stay standing and it was only by God's grace that I wasn't sitting or falling down, right in the middle of the hallway.

Standing erect, eyes boring into all of us, she said, "Now, you will go get your styrofoam cup, your toilet paper and wash cloth, then line up again behind this line to go to the head!" Of course she couldn't just say it, she had to be dramatic and yell it. It didn't take long for me to figure out that the C.O.'s in S.A.I. obviously had no idea how to speak with an indoor voice.

I went back to my cell shaking like jello on a plate, eyeing the bunkbed, wanting so badly to just curl up in a ball and wakeup from this nightmare, enough was enough. I went through the duffel bag, found the wash cloth and toilet paper and…oh my, I can't believe this. In my effort to pick up my duffel bag, I had left my styrofoam cup back in the intake area! *Breathe Mary, Breathe!* The very same cup that only hours before, I had vowed to protect with my life! So much for following through! Why me? What was I going to do about this? It certainly was a fine mess I had gotten myself into. Thankfully, as I made my way to the line, I heard one of the other inmates ask the Corporal for a cup and I held my breath waiting to see what was going to happen next. The Corporal glared at her and yelled, "Who else needs a cup?" I raised my hand and she gave me a cup without saying a word. I was so grateful, I thanked God right there, right then. You would think that asking for a styrofoam cup, would be no big deal, however, here, it was turning out that everything was a big deal. Who ever said "Don't sweat the small stuff" obviously had never been here, it appeared that everything was made into a big deal. In fact, I think that whoever said that was delusional, there are big and small "stuffs." When it was my turn to go into the bathroom, I mean head, I was given a small green bar of soap and told to try not to lose this.

That first night, I tried to relax, but my brain just wasn't going to shut down, it was all over the place, not focusing on anything in particular. That wasn't unusual for me, I had trouble sleeping for years. To add to the problem, every hour a C.O. would shine her high powered flashlight into my face, making sure that I was still breathing. I thrashed all night, like a washing machine on the durable cycle. My restless legs were on full energy.

I have to admit, even now, two years later, that night is still taking up space in my brain. The enormity of sitting in prison, in the middle of the night, seemingly alone with lights from outside along the fence streaming in the unshaded windows and being locked in, is really indescribable. I had to fight all day to keep the tears back and finally I lost that battle. I did manage to keep the sobs at a low level. The sounds I heard coming from me were something that I had never experienced before. I had been through a lot of dark times, but this was absolutely the worst! I don't remember ever crying such big tears, being unable to stop. I don't know how long I cried or even when I finally fell asleep.

I woke up to the sound of the C.O.'s screaming at the trainees to get up, get ready and line up for chow. I didn't know what time it was, but the sun wasn't even up yet. I learned later that the trainees were woke up at 5:30 a.m. each morning to the same screaming. It had been quite a night, the sheets and blankets were twisted and turned. The mattress was vinyl on the outside and the flat sheet was rolled up into a ball. The bed was a disaster. How was I ever going to get sleep here? Between the hourly visits, wrestling with the bedding and the nightmares, I just didn't know how I was going to do it and to think I had at least 23 months of this!

There was something I could do and that was to pray, I got down on my arthritic knees and prayed. I asked God to give me the strength to get through this darkness, to be with me in my time of abandonment, at least that is what it felt like. I asked that He open my eyes, ears, and heart to what He wanted me to learn from this ordeal. I asked for His patience with me, as my mind so easily strayed, making praying all the harder.

After the trainees had gone upstairs for chow, which was housed within the unit, I heard the jingling of keys and the door to my cell opened with the C.O. telling me to get my cup, toilet paper, soap, along with my wash cloth and line up for my turn to use the head and to get water and return to my cell. Standing in line, I was about to speak to the woman in front of me when I heard, "There is to be no talking." It was obvious that after spending our first night in S.A.I. we had a few things to say.

It seemed as though you were rushed to do everything only to stand in line and wait. For the past two years, I hadn't stood for any length of time, my muscles certainly had no stamina for it. My neuropathy caused a lot of stabbing pain and of course my knees were throbbing, becoming unbearable. I wondered when I was going to get to go for my healthcare screening and mental evaluation. I needed my medications! I was concerned about the deteriation of both body and mind. In fact, I felt as though my mental state was deteriating faster than my physical state. My body was using my energy just to stay alert in order to obey the rules, many of which I didn't know and to stay alert to possible danger. It was my hope to obey the rules, fly under the radar and leave here in better shape than I came in.

Because we were in quarantine, we weren't allowed to go to the chow hall, our trays were delivered to our cells by the food service workers and after we ate, they would come back around and pick up the trays. After breakfast we were herded to the showers with the same gusto as earlier. Each of us were given a Breck shampoo packet. I hadn't seen that brand since I was a young girl. It smelled like I remembered and actually did a great job on my hair. It felt like the minute we got into the showers we were being screamed at to hurry up and get dressed.

I look back on the five days I spent on the S.A.I. a never ending nightmare. During that time, I was so traumatized, my PTSD was off the chart with my hypervigilance, causing more stress and anxiety that I had ever felt before. I was jumping out of my skin and I could feel the adrenaline coursing through my body. To make matters worse, I wasn't eating and I wasn't eliminating my intake of fluids. I remember looking at my ankles and they were very swollen. I have always been sensitive to noise, loud voices and unexpected sounds. The trainees were on the go from 5:30 am until 10:00 pm each night. Between the staff barking orders, berating the trainees and the trainee's responses of "Ma'am, Yes Ma'am, Ma'am, no Ma'am," I thought I would lose my mind.

That first day, the staff let us, the quarantines, know that we were privileged to be on their wing, that they had not been consulted or asked to house us there and were unwanted, a distraction to their program. They actually said they could not wait until we were gone. I laughed to myself when I heard that, I couldn't wait to be gone from their wing either.

It was obvious to me that while I was housed there, there wasn't going to be any help for me. I was in their control for everything from the use of the head, to eating, when to dress, when to undress, when to clean our cells and even when we could talk.

On the third day, we were cleared of T.B. which allowed us to go to the day room upstairs, for one hour. The room had a small library, microwaves, tables, pop machine, the store kiosk and the Jpay system that works like the internet for corresponding with the outside world. It was there that I found a copy of OUR DAILY BREAD. It was almost like I was drawn to see it. I remember when I was a child at the Methodist church, my mom had been given THE UPPER ROOM. Thinking back now, I don't think I ever saw her read it. I remember thinking at that time that only little old ladies were carrying it with them. I remembered smiling to myself, now I was a little old woman, well maybe not so little, carrying around OUR DAILY BREAD.

OUR DAILY BREAD, as odd as it sounds, gave me comfort by just holding it in my hand. I was so grateful for having found it and excited to again read God's word. I actually read every day that I had missed in addition to the daily readings. I remembered that the Berrien County jail would not let the prisoners being transferred to prison to take their Bible. The release paperwork that I signed to be transferred to WHV, clearly stated that MDOC would allow personal Bibles to be admitted. This was a point of contention with the inmate "riding out" with me. When we left that morning, she wanted to take her Bible and the Deputy would not let her. She knew her rights and argued the point, but the Deputy wouldn't budge. In talking with other inmates, I learned that there were other counties allowing the prisoners to bring their Bibles. As I saw it, Berrien County was denying prisoners their rights on this issue.

The Bible wasn't just a source of comfort for me, it was a life line, like a ring that is tossed to someone drowning. I knew that it also served as a life line to others. Many women used the Bible to store addresses and phone numbers. I knew the inmate that rode in with me, had her contact's information written down. If you have ever been in extreme duress, you know that your memory can fail you when you need it the most.

To relieve stress during my time in quarantine, I started to journal with paper from the packet that I was given at intake. Most of what I wrote were my conversations with

God, my only constant in life. He has always loved me, unconditionally, something that I never experienced with anyone else. The source of my joy and peace has been that ongoing relationship. I don't know how I would have survived the trials, darkness in my life without Him by my side. Sadly, I had lost hope, joy and peace. I prayed to Him, but looking back, I was not in relationship with Him. I had asked for a greater intimacy with Him, which was my greatest desire. I knew that if I was going to not only survive this, but thrive, He was the only way. I had faith that He would get me through this. I have heard the saying, "If He leads you to it, He will get you through it" which was comforting in itself.

My brain wasn't shutting down which gave me plenty of time to ponder the reason I was there, trying to make sense of the insanity of it all. I knew that this must have been a part of God's plan, I just couldn't see what He intended me to get out of this experience. I trusted Him, I knew at some point I was going to learn a valuable lesson, but in the meantime, I was to be patient. Patience isn't something that comes easy for me on a good day, let alone in survivor mode. It would all become crystal clear when I was ready to accept it and now wasn't that time. With my hope gone, my energy was being used for survival. I was angry, I was sad, I was in disbelief and I was suicidal.

The only relief from all this pain would be to end my life. I was scared about the next 23 months in there and scared about my life when I got out of there. Starting over as a felon wasn't going to be easy. Financially, it would be tough, my life as a financial advisor was over. I would have to live with being labeled a felon and I had no idea how my family and friends were going to accept this or how they were going to treat me. I was struggling to accept that and struggling just to breathe and I was exhausted from sleep deprivation.

After five days on the S.A.I. wing, we were called to pack up, there were rooms for us upstairs. Each of us would be moved to a wing, which would be our "home" for the next 30-45 days until we would be released to the general population, a move that couldn't happen until someone was released to provide an opening in a cell. While I was relieved to be leaving Hades, my anxiety went through the roof…the unknown and I was going to have a roommate and be housed with prisoners from all risk levels.

CHAPTER 3

YOU DON'T MATTER

I the Lord have called thee in righteousness, and will hold thine hand, and will keep thee, and give thee for a covenant of the people, for a light of the gentiles. To open the blind eyes, to bring out the prisoners from the prison, and them that sit in darkness out of the prison house.
- Isaiah 42:6-7

I will sing to you among the nations: for your mercy Reaches unto the heavens, and your truth unto the clouds. Be exalted, O God, above the heavens; let your glory be above all of the earth. O Lord my God, in you I put my trust; save me from all those who persecute me, and deliver me, lest they tear me like a lion, rendering me in pieces, while there is none to deliver.

O Lord my God, if I have done this: if there is iniquity in my hands, if I have repaid evil to him that at peace with me, or have plundered my enemy without cause, let the enemy pursue

me and overtake me; yes, let him trample my life to the earth,
and lay my honor in the dust
- Psalm 7:1-5 NKJV

As I walked down the hallway and up the stairs, I struggled. With one hand on the railing to help my balance and the other hand gripped to the strap of the duffel bag, I took one stair at a time until I finally reached the base, where the Officers were and where I would learn where I was going to bunk. I waited my turn behind the red line, a line that gave the Officers a little more room from the prisoners. I was told that I would house on the D wing. Great, here I was, my first and only time in prison and right off the bat, I was going to be housed with the (P.V's) parole violators. Because of the overcrowding, MDOC was putting prisoners where ever there was room.

I slowly turned around and faced the stairs going up to the floor. I sighed and started to drag my duffel bag across the lobby and towards the stairs. Just as I was about to reach for the railing, one of my fellow inmates from intake, came rushing down the stairs and grabbed the duffel bag's strap and asked if she could help me with it? I was at a loss for words that someone had noticed me, that they were able to see that I needed help. I walked up the stairs behind her and down the long hallway to my cell, which of course had to be the farthest way from the bathroom and the base. I was so grateful for the help. This inmate was the first person to show compassion. I thanked her and God for sending me someone who could assist me in the hour of my need.

So, there I was, on the next leg of my journey. Breathing hard, my body aching all over, exhausted from the lack of sleep and just wanting to lay down and have a moment of peace. That wasn't going to happen! I had been assigned to the top bunk, didn't they know that I was disabled? When I was being held at the county jail, I had been assigned to the top bunk also, but without any ladder, I had positioned my mattress on the floor and stayed there until my Bunkie left and I took her lower bunk. That certainly wasn't going to happen here, there wasn't room.

My new cellmate was a P.V. and from a neighboring city to mine. She told me she had been here for 70 days because of the overcrowding! She was waiting for a bunk to open up so she could be re-assigned and she was praying that it would be tomorrow. She told me that due to the overcrowding, it was getting harder to get a lower bunk. Which of course meant that if you needed a lower bunk, you were going to wait longer to be assigned to the general population. The T.V. rooms were being converted into 10-16 bed cells, storage closets and offices were also being turned into 8-10 bed cells.

What concerned me the most was that violent offenders in some cases were being housed with non-violent offenders. I asked her why there was so much over-crowding. She said that offenders were coming back over and over for violating their parole and many with new charges. The legal system in Michigan had also taken a hard stance on crime including white paper crimes. In addition to that, drug use, especially opiates, was on the rise which resulted in more crime. I told her that when I was paroled, I would do what it took to never come back, in fact, I probably would never leave my home, not wanting to be in the wrong place at the wrong time. There just wasn't any way I was coming back!

As I unpacked my duffel bag, she showed me how to utilize the space in the locker. Since this wasn't her first "rodeo," after serving nine years the first time, she knew the in's and outs and would filling me in. While she served her time, a male guard had raped her repeatedly along with four other women. The women had sued MDOC and actually won! She and the other women received a large settlement yearly, spaced over five years. I didn't ask what she was in for this time and what she had been in for the last time. I figured if she wanted me to know, she would tell me.

As it turned out, my bunkie was a Christian woman and loved to pray and talk about the Lord. Since I didn't have a Bible, so she shared her's with me and we prayed together. I got back to unpacking and thanked God that once again, He had sent me an angel in my time of need, the second one that day! My bunkie was a little disappointed, she thought that today was the day she was going to be moved. I laughed and told her that God knew I would need help, so she would have to wait one more day. She smiled at that and boy, did she have a beautiful smile! I sensed a little bit of her anxiety had gone away, however, it didn't lessen her desire to be moved.

I was exhausted, my energy had tapped out the hour before. I stood before the bunk's ladder, one rung at a time would get me to a place of rest. There were only three rungs, with a lot space between each one and with each one, I struggled. I finally navigated the trek up, collapsed, exhausted on the mattress and just looked out the window, which was so depressing. The re-bar on the windows reminded me that I was in prison and the tattered rag that hung on the window pretending to be a curtain looked like something right out of a horror movie. It was actually held up by three twist ties. It had long since served its useful purpose, now it was just there with no function to it. It was obvious by looking around that the prison was run down, sending the message that its occupants were of no value, that the rundown facility was good enough for us, we didn't matter. I wondered if the Michigan residents knew what was going on here or if they cared. As a Michigan resident, I knew that I had never given any thought to the prison or its prisoners.

I didn't need to be reminded that I didn't matter here, that my only use or value for MDOC was a body to be counted for reimbursement. I was told they were reimbursed

$35,000 per inmate and $40,000 for inmates needing ongoing medication, which I did or hopefully would soon. I knew that my slowed movement was due to not having my medication for over two weeks. From somewhere I heard my name, FAHER being called. It was an officer downstairs at the base. I tried as hard as I could to get down that ladder, which was risky business, down the hallway and down the stairs, but obviously, I wasn't fast enough. The officer yelled my name again, this time even louder. To add to my anxiety, there was a prisoner with the name of Farrer, which sounded to me like Faher, making me question who was actually being called. The officers had no idea how hard I was trying to be compliant and actually, they didn't care.

I talked to the C.O. about needing a bottom bunk and she asked me if I had a bottom bunk detail? Obviously not…I had no idea what she was talking about. Evidently, when I had met with a P.A. and gave him my medical history, what medications that I took and about my disability, he should have automatically given me a bottom bunk detail along with a no stairs detail. A detail is the official paper that would give me those rights. Since I was new to the system, I had a lot to learn. I asked what I had to do to rectify the situation and she told me that I would have to "kite" medical, that I needed an appointment to discuss my need for the details. I was to learn that kiting is the only way to get anything done. In most cases, it seemed that it took a few days or weeks to get any response. After writing the kite, I wondered how long it was going to take to see the P.A. or if I was going to have to pay $5.00 for the appointment, the co-pay if it wasn't a regularly scheduled appointment. So with that, I had to resign myself to going up and down that ladder, of course with much dread.

Sleep was still illusive, nowhere to be found. I had trouble falling asleep and once I was asleep, staying asleep. I knew that I wasn't getting to the REM stage which was critical to sleeping. It didn't help that my size 8x pajama's kept falling down and practically strangling me due to all the tossing and turning. Overcrowding meant that clothes in the right sizes were mostly unavailable. Intake didn't have my correct size in a few things. I felt like a clown in the bottoms, I could pull them up to my nose! Added to all that, the radiator heat rose up to the ceiling, making it intolerable, suffocating and even with the window open all night. The early spring morning breeze seemed to just sink to the bottom bunk, which was alright with my bunkie, she liked it cool. A few of the nights, in between the hourly bed checks, I snuck down the ladder and laid on the cement floor or sat in the desk chair to cool off.

> *Be merciful to me, O God, be merciful to me! For my soul trusts in you; and in the shadow of your wings I will make my refuge, until these calamities have passed by.*

I will cry out to the God most high, to God who performs all things for me; He reproaches the one who would swallow me up.

God shall send forth His mercy and His truth. My soul is among the lion; I lie among the sons of men who are set on fire, whose teeth are spears and arrows, and their tongue a sharp sword.

Be exalted, O God, above the heavens; let your glory be above all the earth. They have prepared a net for my steps; my soul is bowed down; they have dug a pit before me; into the midst of it they themselves have fallen. My heart is steadfast, O God, my heart is steadfast; I will sing and give praise.
- **Psalm 57**

During those quiet moments when it seemed the prison was asleep and even a few of the officers were too, I felt the closest to God. I cried out for Him and always felt His presence. My mind was still racing on about what had happened, still questioning how it happened and in addition to the evil that I felt was pursuing me.

In getting real with myself, I had been so engrossed with what, I felt was done to me and during that time I hadn't been taking my troubles to God. Yes, of course I asked Him to be with me in my time of need and I believed that He was, however, never did I pray to Him for help. I didn't pray for Him to do His will, it was always, my will and we all know how that turned out. I am now ashamed that I hadn't trusted Him more and believed that He could have made a difference in my life. I needed my medication, I didn't know how much longer I could hold it together without it. Did I ask God to help me with that? We all know the answer to that…no. God was my go-to when I was lonely and afraid, I had never relied on Him for anything but to be there when I needed or wanted Him. In fact, I was not in an intimate relationship with Him, I longed for something more but was clueless as to what "it" was. I knew that He loved me unconditionally and would never forsake me, He told me so, all those years ago. I felt like a child, abandoned, lost and crying out from the desert for someone, anyone to help me.

I can't think of a time when my hypervigilance wasn't on full alert! I had learned a few meditation techniques that did help, in fact, I was able to take a few meditation classes while I was in prison. I cherished those times, because I felt free, like I wasn't incarcerated. Yes, God had seen me through the darkness only to see me enter into the vortex, again.

It wouldn't be until much later, with the help of my therapist and psychiatrist that I would learn, accept and acknowledge that I had been in trouble long before all of this had happened. That my failed marriages would lead to my undoing or as I now know, my rebirth. It seemed that I had been unraveling since 2004 when I was divorced from my first husband of over 25 years. It took group counseling, individual counseling and a psychiatrist to diagnose me with Complex PTSD in addition to my chronic depression.

I was so stressed and one of the things that stressed me the most was not being able to communicate with my family and friends. As much as I was clueless about everything, since this was my first time, it was also the first time for my family and friends to have someone they knew in prison, they were clueless as to what they could be doing. I hoped that they were dazed and befuddled about the situation and not just dismayed and going with the flow. I already had learned that I needed to be proactive here, when it came to my mental and physical health and they needed to be proactive to find out what it is that families can do to assist an inmate. One thing I had learned is that with so many of the inmates having been here before, their family and friends knew exactly they could do. For example, how to put money in the Jpay (Computer system) account so that the inmate could make purchases on the "store," again, a computerized system. It also acted like e-mail so that you could send messages and receive messages. I needed to send a letter, as soon as possible, asking for all of the phone numbers and addresses that I might need.

It seemed to me that the P.V.'s hit the dirt landing right side up, they were off and running while I was still waiting to de-plane. I just couldn't understand why my family wasn't trying to find out what they could do and just do it. My biggest problem was that I didn't know what I didn't know.

My feelings of being abandoned by my family and friends was so severe it was actually turning into anger, why weren't they helping me? Anger seemed to be gnawing at my insides, it was no wonder that my mental and physical health were deteriating at such an alarming rate. I knew that anger was dangerous, it was something I had always bottled up and I needed to do that in here, my survival depended on that.

My hypervigilance skyrocketed to Pluto and beyond. The shock of accepting what had happened was too much on so many different levels.

We all have defining moments in our lives and I have had many, too many, but nothing compared to this, nothing! It shattered my already glued together mirror, a mirror that was functional and fragile and would never be unbroken.

CHAPTER 4

OVERLOAD

Awake my glory! Awake lute and harp! I will awaken the dawn. I will, praise you, O Lord, among the peoples; I will sing to you among the nations: for your mercy Reaches unto the heavens, and your truth unto the cloud. Be exalted, O God, above the heavens; let your glory be above all of the earth.
- Psalm 57

Since my brain was not shutting down, I was awake all night, again, flashes of my past kept showing up and some of them were terrifying nightmares. I think this defining moment on my journey had been the hammer, smashing the well-polished veneer, letting the light into the cracks, dark places I had never allowed myself to visit. The biggest problem being, everything was jamming the brain at the same time, causing OVERLOAD!

Imagine yourself on a tilt-a-whirl at the county fair and it starts to move in unsynchronized movements....nauseous, breathless, not knowing where to focus, wishing it would all just stop. This is my definition of OVERLOAD.

Not only was I dealing with the new challenges of prison life, both overt and covert, but all of the unresolved issues of my past. Issues that I thought had been resolved were now getting a second look. For too long, I tried to convince myself that I had dealt with everything and everyone. Actually what I had done was to intellectualize everything, thus making everything make sense so that I could live with myself and others. What I actually was doing was shoving everything into a bag that I was carrying on my back. It certainly was heavy, reeking and no composting was going on. Put another way, I wasn't actually dealing with a lot of things.

I prayed to God to give me the strength and courage that I would need to cope with this part of my journey and to give me an open mind and heart to hear and listen to what path God would like me to take, not my will, but His will. In all honesty, I don't remember ever praying that way before. My life up to this point had been all about Mary, Mary's will and God could come along for the ride. I prayed:

"Lord, Creator of all, please lead me where you need me and let me be an instrument of Your truth, peace, light and love." Amen

After two days, my bunkie was finally given orders to pack up, she was moving on up to the west side, where she had been housed before. The west side is where the prisoners evaluated with higher risk factors were housed. She was so happy, she was dancing and praising Jesus. She was beaming, her smile could light up a dark room! She didn't have much time and as she was about out of the door, I wished her well and asked God to be with her.

She had only been gone for a few minutes when my new Bunkie showed up. The overcrowding had put so much stress on the housing system to "move'm out and move'm in," that the filling of beds was done in a matter of minutes, literally.

My new bunkie, come to find out, wasn't her first rodeo either. After she unpacked and got settled in, we would have time to chat. It was always a priority to unpack and leave nothing in the duffel bag, you could be charged with escaping if they found anything in it. I had to laugh at that, I could visualize myself escaping, throwing my bag over the coiled barbed wire fence first before attempting to get over and land all in one piece. I can tell you this, if I ever thought that I was going to escape, my bag would be the last thing that I would take with me!

She was here for a parole violation along with a new charge. She had absconded for three months by cutting off her tether. (Ankle Home Monitoring Device) She was going to have to wait until the parole board met and made a decision as to whether she would just get more probation, possibly with community service or whatever the board would deem necessary or a "flop," (More prison time). It seemed that God had blessed me again, she loved the Lord!

She could see me struggle each time I went up and down that ladder. It wasn't just the arthritis pain, it was my lack of balance and strength to navigate up, hauling the mass of weight. She even volunteered to trade bunks, however, the C.O.'s said no, that I couldn't be moved until my bottom bunk detail was issued from the medical department…I wasn't going anywhere!

In unit 9, the chow hall was in the building, not far to walk for meals. I was still worried about having to walk there just to stand in line. In the general population, the chow hall was in a separate building and depending on which unit you were assigned to, the distance from it would vary, the only thing that was a guarantee was from whichever unit you came from, there would be the long lines.

The tables in Unit 9's chow hall were stainless steel set up like rows of picnic tables. They worked for most people, however, if you were obese, they were a nightmare and no exceptions were made to accommodate you. My problem was that I not only was fat, but that I had very little strength in my legs to lift them up and the arthritis made it difficult to bend my knees. To add to the nightmare, settling in had to be done quickly as the next inmate was waiting to sit down. I have to say in all fairness, the other prisoners were gracious and never were unkind about it.

I hated going to the chow hall, it felt like the minute you settled in to eat, you were being yelled at to eat, no talking, and move on. I have never been a fast eater, my mother had driven that into me at an early age. I never had enough time to eat everything off of my tray, even if I had wanted to. It was forbidden to take any food to the cell. If you were caught, you would be "ticketed" for stealing MDOC property. Sad to say, but a lot of food was trashed because people didn't have time to eat it and if someone was hungry, you couldn't give them what you didn't want, and that was forbidden too. Everything was cooked like at a nursing home, without seasoning, including salt, very bland and you had to make a choice between a fruit or dessert, you couldn't have both.

At intake, I had filled out the questionnaire that had asked what my goal was for my time spent here and I had listed, lose weight. It certainly was going to be easier than I thought, the food was not appetizing, and there wasn't enough of it. My goal to lose weight and be the best version of myself when I walked out of those gates was getting a big help from the kitchen. Between the stress of the last two years and my deteriating health, eating sweets to help me numb out, my drug of choice, I had put on one hundred pounds, making matters worse. That one hundred pounds is what I had vowed to lose to become the best version of myself when I walked through those gates to freedom. I was determined to make this dark period on my journey have meaning, or as King Solomon would say, it was all vanity.

We were allotted one hour of recreation time out of the cell each day. Our choices were to going outside or going to the day room, which housed a television, the kiosk, electronic store, the electronic email system called Jpay. Since our family and friends had to initiate the first email, making that first contact, I would have to write them and tell them about the system. So I knew it was going to take a little extra time. It was frustrating and I was so depressed about not having any way to be connected. I felt so alone. To cheer me up, another inmate said that my family could go to the MDOC's website and learn what they could do for their felon. I didn't think that they would be proactive and they weren't. About every three days, we could use the phone, which of course I couldn't figure out how to use and my biggest problem being that it seemed that my hearing had deteriated to a level that made phone use, next to impossible, with the noise in the hallways.

There were lines for the jpay, (computer system, for messaging family and friends.) It seemed like everyone else had family and friends anxious to make contact. It helped that most of the women were "repeaters" and were able to use their previous jpay accounts with all of the contacts already connected. In addition to the jpay kiosk, there was a "store" kiosk (computer system to order personals and food.) I had some money on my account which was transferred along with me from the county jail. There was so much to be done in that hour and too many people trying to get it done. The other twenty three hours of the day were spent in our cell with the exception of bathroom use and going to the chow hall. If you were lucky, you had "call outs" to go somewhere.

Every morning I was called out to a trailer located next to the unit for my daily medications, "med lines." The trailer also housed a dental office and medical rooms for Unit 9. That was where my P.A. was located. Physically, I didn't know how I was going to make it here, not to mention emotionally. It seemed everything was to hurry up, just to stand in line. My tolerance for standing in line was shaky at best.

There were a few feral cats which lived under the trailer and several inmates would smuggle food out to them. Even with prison food, they were scrawny. Later on, I too would be one of the inmates to feed the kitties. I knew that if I was caught, there would be consequences, however, I was willing to risk that. I am a devout cat lover and just because I was in prison didn't mean that my compassion was going to be turned off. One cat in particular let me pet her and I got to talk to her, it reminded me that I had fur babies being taken care of, waiting for my return. There was my calico cat, Tia, Lil Bob, a beautiful black cat and Buddha, a Tibetan spaniel. I really tried not to think about them, wondering what they were thinking, how they were getting along, did they miss me? When I did think about them, my heart would break and tears would quickly follow. They had been my constant companions for quite some time and it really bothered me to think that they would think that I had abandoned them. I knew all too well how it felt to be abandoned and it was more than I could take thinking that they felt that way.

I have always been an animal lover, cats in particular. Even as a small girl, my cats would be the comfort that I ran to when life became more than I could bear. After my divorce from my second husband, my friends encouraged me to get a dog and give up on men. It is funny to say that, but I now understand the reasoning behind that statement. Buddha is loyal, trusting, likes the way I look in the morning and doesn't seem to mind my bad breath. He always returns unconditional love even when I might not be as loving as I should be. Of course everyone knows that DOG spelt backwards is GOD, not that there is any comparison, but it is something to think about. I was so blessed to have friends that were taking care of my "fur family."

Another "pet" that hung around the trailer was a Canadian goose named Ping Ping. I was told it was a male, which confused me because he sat on a nest made of stones next to the electric fence. He never left it and sat proudly on it even in the pouring rain. One day that I went to the trailer to get my meds, Ping Ping was gone. I was told that earlier that day, a C.O. had brought a dog in and they disposed of the eggs. Now, in the free world, that might not have been as big of deal as it was in here. Many of the inmates were able to show their compassion for life by their devotion to the various animals here and when something happened to any of them, many were devastated, including me.

CHAPTER 5

HOT, HOT, HOT

The Lord shall judge the peoples; Judge me, O Lord, according to my righteousness, and according to my integrity within me. Oh, let the wickedness of the wicked come to an end, but establish the just, for the righteous God test the hearts and minds. My defense is of God, who saves the upright in heart.
- **Psalms 7:8-10**

Finally, I got to see the P.A. and he gave me a bottom bunk detail. If only he could have done that to begin with! I had been having trouble with my balance and asked him if I could have a cane or walker, I was worried about walking and standing in line, once I got moved over to the general population. He said no, that wasn't going to happen, that the prison did not recognize my disability. He also said no when I requested a no stair detail. I knew that some of the units had second stories. I was angry, one more thing to have to endure and again, that was an emotion that would have to be buried.

When I got back to the unit, I handed over my bottom bunk detail to the C.O. on duty at the base, she just stared at me with no comment. I was excited to tell, my bunkie that we were finally going to be able to switch bunks. When I got back to the cell and told her, she just stared at me. While I had been at my appointment, she had gone to see her P.A. and she was given a bottom bunk detail due to her carpel tunnel. Strange, she had never mentioned to me that she had carpel tunnel. I was flabbergasted to say the least. I knew what that meant, I was going to be moved to another cell so that I could have a bottom bunk. I was saddened at the prospect and overjoyed to know that I could get in and out of bed without having to worry about falling. I have never been one who adapted to change well and in prison, it was a skill that I would need to improve on. So, I thanked God for giving me good bunkies so far and knew that He would be with me again. I knew that it would be like a roll of the dice, there were more than not, unbalanced, scary people, not to mention all of the "studs" with their messy he/she business.

The day after I received the bottom bunk detail paperwork, I got called to the base, which of course meant down the long hallway and steps and as usual, a yell to hurry up. As I made my way down, I remember thinking that a positive aspect to the move might be that I would be moved closer to the base and the bathrooms. I was ordered to pack up, I was being moved across the hall from my current cell. I was going to switch places with the women in the bottom bunk, who did not have a bottom bunk detail. As I got to my cell, my new bunkie learned about the switch and I heard her kicking the door and screaming her displeasure about the move. I was so shocked at her immature behavior and grateful when several other inmates on the hall yelled that they would be glad to have me as a bunkie and that she was being rude.

My new bunkie was 21 and was very proud of herself, she couldn't wait to tell me that she was in there for trying to rob her drug dealer and threatening her co-defendant when he starting talking. Well, I guess two out of three wasn't all bad. I was positive that God had a reason and that I would soon find out what it was. God had blessed me so far and in blessing me, maybe I was to be a blessing to her, after all, I prayed daily for Him to lead me where He needed me.

It wasn't easy to share a small cell with her, not only were our age's far apart, but about in everything else we were universes apart. Actually, come to think about it, I don't think we had anything in common. I just wanted to be left alone in a drama free cell, a cell that was quiet and could be a haven in the harsh environment of prison.

She loved to sit on the upturned trash can next to the open door and talk to anyone who walked by and whoever would listen. It was something that was against the rules and if she was caught, we both could be censored. I talked to her about it and she told me it was my fault, that I was always sleeping or reading, not giving her any company. It was hard not to laugh out loud, I just had to remember that she was young and had low self-esteem, was still jumpy due to coming off of her drug addictions and I was just going to have to put up with her, pray for her and continue on.

Instead of getting high on drugs, she was getting high on DRAMA! This was her first time in prison and everything was fair game for her. I told her not to get involved with the he/she thing, that it would only bring drama and trouble into her life. Drama and trouble that could affect her ability to go home on her ERD (Early Release Date). She obviously had no desire to listen to me. I caught on when she was passing notes with another young gal. I just couldn't understand it, she had a son that she had adopted out and several boyfriends. I had heard the term, gay for the stay....I wondered, was that it?

One day, standing in the chow line, an inmate from across the hall told me she had heard my bunkie talking to the Unit ARUM (Area Residential Unit Supervisor) about needing a new cellmate. My first reaction was not only stunned but hurt by her actions. As soon as she came back to the cell, I asked her about her conversation with the ARUM. She stared at me and instantly started to yell at the room across the hall at the woman that had told me about the incident. Obviously she must have seen her walking by as she was talking. I asked her what had just happened, what had precipitated her actions.

After she calmed down enough to talk, she admitted to the conversation she had with the ARUM asking for a new bunkie, she went on to say that she had did it for me, knowing that I would be happier. I just hate it when someone says that their actions are for me. Anyway, she went on to say that she knew that being with someone closer to my own age would be better and that she hadn't said anything negative about me, as if that made it all right. I remember wanting to laugh and having a very hard time just listening and not saying what I really thought. The unspoken reason of course was that she wanted someone closer to her age, someone to drag into her drama, someone who could understand and appreciate her "generation" and life style. Most importantly, she wanted someone who would pass contraband, get high with her and definitely not someone who was always reminding her of the rules!

As soon as she was done talking, I finally allowed myself to laugh and told her this wasn't college, she wasn't going to be able to pick her "roommates." For a few days after that drama, the cell was icier with each of us avoiding each other and in a small space that two people are cooped up in for twenty three hours a day, it wasn't easy.

Store day! Pandemonium... Every two weeks, the inmates that were allowed to order a "store" consisting of food, hygiene products and a few miscellaneous items had them delivered to the unit. From the minute I got up, I could feel the excitement echoing from the hallway. As time would go on, I would learn that life in prison rotated around store day. Each housing unit had a different day and that there were a couple of men that were in charge of the deliveries, also in charge of delivering the quarterly boxes that either the inmate or the inmate's family could order. I couldn't even remember what I had ordered with the money that had transferred over from the county jail. Everything is ordered two weeks prior on the kiosk (store) located in the day room.

A lot of the excitement was due to items that family members had ordered for their inmate in the boxes. The atmosphere almost felt like the anticipation of a Christmas morning. To add to the frenzied fury, store day brought out the hustle in a lot of the prisoners, almost like a hive of activity, trading items mainly to pay off debts incurred since the last store. Commerce is alive and well in the prison system. I read somewhere that before prison's banned cigarettes, cigarettes were the currency, today it was the Ramon noodle, three packs equaled one dollar. You would be surprised at what a bar of soap would buy, especially a few days before the next store. As I observed the action, it occurred to me that some people were just trading to trade, it was addicting and it filled their need for a high. My cellmate was no exception, she traded to trade. There were some real sharks out there. I learned that when I got to my unit on grounds just how much of a hustle it all really was. There were two for one stores, cashing in on the wants of an inmate…usually it involved sugar, cookies, candy bars and the king of kings, a chocolate Hunny Bun, a whopping 690 calories!

Trading is strictly forbidden and the C.O.'s knew that it was going to happen and the only question was how much energy they wanted to expend that day. If you were caught with something that you did not have a receipt for, you were "busted." The items were considered contraband and usually confiscated and the inmate would get a "ticket" resulting in a L.O.P., (Loss of Privileges), for example a number of days without the phone, use of the day room or outside recreation time. In other wards being confined to the cell and only being allowed out for the bathroom and the chow hall and mandatory call outs. If you were called for a non-mandatory callout, like yoga, you couldn't go. If the L.O.P. time was longer than three weeks, you would run the risk of losing the privilege of going back to that class, as three misses usually got you thrown out of a class. Not all C.O.'s treated store day the same, some were okay with it if you didn't do it in front of them and there were others that couldn't wait to bust you, it's like they were just as excited about store days as the inmates but for different reasons.

Everyone was encouraged to keep their receipts so that if your cell was shook down, you could prove you bought the item(s) in question.

I watched my bunkie wheeling and dealing, just to do it. She wasn't very good at it, as she usually traded for something of lesser value. I already could identity the sharks, the pros who knew exactly what they were doing. As it was, she obviously had the store "fever" and couldn't be talked out of trading or even to wait a day or two.

Two days after store day, I went down to the base to ask for shampoo, as I hadn't received my box with the hygiene products that I had requested to be bought. Obviously, my son hadn't received that information. Of course, the C.O. on duty was the vilest…she informed me that since we had received store a few days ago, I should have ordered what I needed and I would no longer be able to use MDOC's products. To make matters worse, she couldn't just tell me, she had to yell at me with her ghetto mouth. At that point in time, I was so angry about what I felt was injustice done to me and this just added to that huge list of what I was ready to explode about.

It was bad enough that all of my rights had been stripped away, but I had to be reminded daily that I was the property of MDOC and have to listen to the C.O.'s yell, scream and demean me, it was so unbearable. I wondered, is this how the Marines broke down their new recruits so they could build them up the way that they wanted?

To add to my anger and angst, the judicial system, thought that I belonged here. That I deserved to be treated this way, less than human. My life for the last three years had spiraled out of control and what could go wrong, often did. For example, I had sent a letter to my home address (living there since 1999) to the person living there that was taking care of my beloved pets and the property. In the letter, I had asked him to contact my friend Jan and give her my contact information and also that I needed her contact information. I also wanted to have her add money to my account here so that I could make an order for the next store. Everything was time sensitive. I had also included in the letter information about how to have a box, which could only be ordered quarterly, sent to me. Talk about being frustrated, having the feeling that I was in the dead zone…the letter was returned back to me from the Stevensville Post Office, stamped, NOT DELIVERABLE AS ADDRESSED! I read and re-read that envelope over and over and it WAS properly addressed! What was going on here? What was happening to me? I felt abandoned, adding to my feeling of hopelessness. I cried out to God to hear me, I needed Him, I knew that He was in here with me.

I had heard through inmate.com (the grapevine for gossip) that RGC had never been like this before. That what I was experiencing was something different that any of the P.V.'s had experienced on prior lock-ups. The explanation given to me was that the new warden, who had taken over only a few months ago was determined to lower the number of repeaters. It was his opinion that prison must be too comfortable of a place that people wanted to come back and he was going to change that! In all due respect, he probably was on to something, most of the P.V.'s that I had met, seemed to be glad to be back. They hit the ground running as if they had never left. Once back, they were so seasoned, that the hustle, the he/she games and manipulating other inmates and expecting to also manipulate the staff, actually thinking that some of the staff were their buddies. The C.O.'s were definitely running with the new agenda, and being buddies didn't seem part of the plan. I couldn't imagine ever doing anything that would bring me back to this place.

I found that as the days were going by, I was spending more and more time in my cell. My energy level had continued to seep from my body with no stoppage. My tolerance to the noise and always being surrounded by people was almost paralyzing. My energy was continuing to further drain me, leaving me feeling as if my very essence was evaporating. I remember asking myself over and over, how had this happened?

On introspection, I have noticed the need to hibernate after being subjected to the crowds; everything from family gatherings, concerts to just being at a mall. I have always enjoyed my solitude and actually enjoy my own company. I have always thought of that it was the result of being an only child, how I was wired.

One of the advantages of store day was that for a few days there was a frenzy of activity cooking and that also meant getting to sample new recipes. I never knew that ramen noodles could be prepared in so many different ways. The library actually had several cookbooks on cooking in prison, who would have ever thought about that!

My bunkie decided that I needed to experience and be educated on prison "cook-ups." I had no idea what to expect. My only knowledge about ramen noodles was when my son had told me about them, he used them in college. The recipe that she used was one that she had used in her county jail. Using a soft tortilla, she crunched up chili ramen noodles, spicy hot chips, a dill pickle and salami (all purchased or traded for at the store). She folded them into the tortilla, wrapped it in the plastic bag that the tortilla's came in and then put it under her mattress for twenty minutes. She explained to me that if a microwave was available, it could be cooked there for about four minutes. I couldn't see how it was going to work, but it did and it was delicious! Of course it was too hot and spicy for me so I only had a tiny taste. It actually had "cooked". My mouth was on fire, after all, I had been eating food without salt, pepper or any other seasoning. I definitely had taste bud overload. Like so many firsts in my life, I will never forget my first prison "cook-up."

CHAPTER 6

BONA-Fied

I cried unto the Lord with my voice; with my voice unto the Lord did I make my supplication. I poured out my complaint before Him; I shewd before Him my trouble. When my spirit was overwhelmed within me, then thou knewest my path. In the way wherein I walked have they privily laid a snare for me. I looked on my right hand and beheld, but there was no man that would know me: Refuge failed me; no man cared for my soul.

I cried unto thee, O Lord: I said, thou art my refuge and my portion in the land of the living. Attend to my cry; for I am brought very low: Deliver me from my persecutors; for they are stronger than I. Bring my soul out of prison, that I may praise thy name: The righteous shall compass me about; for thou shalt deal bountifully with me.

- Psalm 142

Safety was definitely at the top of my list. In order for me to have some semblance of it, I was spending a lot of time reading, meditating and for the first time since I received it, started reading <u>Our Daily Bread</u>. I didn't have a Bible to cross reference with and prayed to God that He would find a way for me to find one. It wasn't long after that, that during our rec time, in the day room, I was talking to a fellow inmate about God and that I would really like a Bible. She told me she would hunt one down for me and any other materials she could find. She said she volunteered at the chapel. She went on to explain that the new warden was taking a hard stance on drug use and one of the ways to slow down the stream of substances coming in, was to stop all book donations, including the Bible from coming in. I remember thinking to myself, Satan was all over that! The only way to receive a new book or Bible was to have someone on the outside order it from Amazon, an approved vender, and have it sent directly to the prison. It never occurred to me to have my son send me one, I definitely was not thinking clearly. In addition to that, I wanted and needed it now!

The day finally arrived that I decided that if I was in prison, a felon, I needed to be a "bona-fide criminal." I guess it was a ritual of initiation to all the new inmates. At WHV, a crime is anything from passing candy to talking out of the cell door or even passing a roll of toilet paper to someone who needed it. So my bunkie and I gave it some thought and I decided that my "crime" was to pass a book across the hall to a woman from my county. She was an avid reader and needed something to read. I had gotten it from the day room, which had very little to offer. It was all about timing. The C.O.'s had to be occupied elsewhere and not sitting in front of the monitors watching all movement. I thought it would be a cinch since my cell was at the end of a very long hallway. I looked down the hallway towards the stairs and did not see anyone, so as quickly as I could, I slid the book across the floor and it stopped just in front of the door, not going in. Just my luck, not only not sliding it hard enough, a C.O. was coming up the stairs yelling "Who passed that book?" Immediately I heard all the cell doors on the hallway slam shut in unison. It reminded me of turtles pulling their heads back into their shells for safety. The cellmate of the woman that wanted the book was still at the door and she kicked the book so that it would land in between cells, making it impossible to tell who and had slid it and who it was intended for. I tried so hard not to laugh or wet my pants!

Evidently, the C.O. had been looking at the monitor and saw the book moving across the floor, but because of our location at the back of the hall it must have been fuzzy and she could not make out the to and fro. I of course, had not closed the cell door. I could hear all of the laughter coming from the other cells. Everyone knew this was my first attempt to become a bona-fide criminal and had botched it. I was so embarrassed that I failed that I forgot about the consequences of my actions and I knew there would be consequences. As she approached the cell door, she figured that it must have been me, since I was the only one standing in a doorway. I stepped forward and owned up to the crime, however, I stood mute when she asked me who the book was intended for and she already knew I wouldn't answer. I certainly was new to all of this, but I knew that rule number one is never to rat out a fellow inmate and that inmate was safe behind the closed door of her cell laughing.

This C.O. was a seasoned officer and didn't go out of her way to write tickets. Tickets are the consequence of breaking a rule, they take away a prisoner's right to something, anywhere from staying in their cell for 24 hours a day, to sanctions of no phone use, no day room etc. Usually the days of the sanction could be three to thirty. She asked me for my I.D., told me she was going to write a ticket and slowly walked back down the stairs to the base.

I just stood there, already thinking how I was going to become bona-fide and not get caught. What was wrong with me, it seemed everyone else did it all day long and never got caught? It never occurred to me that I didn't need to become bona fide and that this action could start me down the wrong path. My best guess was that God wasn't going to let me go down that path. The cell doors started to slowly open one by one with a few remarks directed my way. I must have still felt emboldened, I put my thumbs to my shirt like I had suspenders on and crowed, and "I am a criminal now, just not bona-fide....yet"

I understood that this type of infraction wouldn't be reported to the parole board, but if a ticket was written up, it would go into my file. I actually wasn't worried about being sanctioned to the cell for any length of time, I rarely left it anyway.

I knew that there was no justification for my actions, I knew that passing the book wasn't allowed, even if it was to be helpful to someone, which if caught there would be consequences. One of the problems in RGC was that the prisoners are locked down for approximately twenty three hours a day and with that much time, reading was a great way for them to pass the time. The library was lacking in books and the books that were there were left overs, I looked at them as books that didn't sell in a yard sale, so they were donated to the prison. The "good" books were taken by prisoners, who with no respect for their fellow inmates, took them with them when they were moved to the general population. The absurdity of that is that all the units on the grounds have their own libraries in addition to the main library.

That evening when med lines were called, I didn't have my I.D., it was sitting on top of the C.O.'s desk. Without an I.D. no meds would be distributed. I thought about my options and there was only one and that was to put on my big girl panties and face the consequences of my actions.

I went down to the base and approached her, standing behind the red line so that I couldn't get too close, took in a breath and apologized for my disrespectful behavior. I explained that I knew when I passed the book that it was in violation of the rules and that it was a poor decision on my part. She kept her eyes solidly on me and without saying a word, slid my I.D. over to me. I thanked her and quickly went to the med line, just to hurry and wait in line.

On my way to the trailer, I was going over my stupidity, knowing that in the next twenty-four hours I would find out if a ticket has been written or not. If I had been a betting woman, I would have betted on her not writing that ticket. I actually would have been surprised if she did. Those twenty-four hours passed and I never heard a thing about it. Lesson learned. It still remained to be seen if I could become a bona-fide criminal.

A few weeks later, the new bunkie in my previous cell let me know that she wanted a state issued button down shirt. She only received pullovers. I had been told that the button downs were hard to come by and I had been issued three of them at intake. All three were a size 5X, which were way too large for me. We negotiated a trade, I would give her my button down for one of her pullovers, actually smaller and would fit me better. Since I wasn't boa-fide yet, I asked my bunkie, who was a pro at passing items to do it for me. I told her not to take any chances, I wasn't in a hurry. She agreed saying it would be no problem. She threw the shirt across the hall and my old bunkie caught it, like the pro's both of them were, but, a C.O. had seen the whole thing go down being the pro that she was! She came down the hall yelling "Who just threw that?" All I could hear from my bunk, were the slamming of cell doors. My bunkie stepped forward and admitted to throwing the shirt. The C.O. asked her if the shirt was hers and she said yes. The C.O. then looked across the hall and my old bunkie was still standing there with her cell door open with the shirt in her hands. The C.O. asked her if that was the shirt, she said yes and gave it to her and as she was taking the shirt, she asked both women for their I.D.'s. My heart sunk, I remember getting that gut feeling of doom. After getting everything she needed, she proceeded to the base downstairs. I must confess, of all of the officers I had met or would meet, she was absolutely the worst. Every word out of her mouth was vile, she was a racist and most definitely unprofessional.

After my bunkie closed the cell door, I told her it wasn't right for her to take the blame for me. My conscience was bothering me and I wanted to set things right, if there was such a thing. She told me in no uncertain terms that it was a bad idea. She went on to say that in telling the truth that the shirt was mine, she would also get in trouble for lying to an officer, making matters worse. I remember feeling, mad, sad and at a loss for the whole situation.

The way the sanction process worked was that another officer had to review the ticket and then go over it with the inmate, giving the inmate the opportunity to protest it. Very few people went that route because that process involved the Area Resident Unit Manager and if she agreed with the ticket, the time was doubled. I had heard of a few inmates "beating" their tickets, however, I knew as well as my bunkie, she wouldn't get that break, she had too many other tickets on file and she also had tangled with this C.O. before.

The next day, the very loud and course C.O. yelled for my bunkie, which of course surprised all of us because we thought that another officer had to review and go over the ticket with her, however, this C.O. wasn't going to let her off that easy. The ticket had been reviewed alright, but this C.O. must have asked to deliver it. Once at the base, my bunkie got the ticket and a contraband violation ticket. The C.O. had noticed that the shirt was a size 5X and my bunkie was definitely a medium. The button down shirt was confiscated and would not be returned as it was contraband. She was asked again, who the shirt belonged to, knowing that the size was not matching up with her. Nothing was ever said, but I felt that the C.O. had to know that it was mine. My bunkie stuck to the original story and that was that.

Later in the evening my bunkie received the paperwork for the ticket. It stated that she had endangered the safety of others by tossing the shirt recklessly across the hall. That was so typical of this C.O. In addition, she received fifteen days of L.O.P. (Loss of privileges), which happened to coincide with the Memorial Day's festivities. It was going to be a long fifteen days!

The next day, if by magic, there was a notice taped under her name on the wall beside our door, detailing the sanction. The only thing positive that came out of the entire ordeal was that my old bunkie didn't get a ticket, which shocked both of us. Obviously this particular C.O. was having too much fun with my bunkie.

I still had two more button down shirts and the inmate that wanted one, still did. This time, however, we handled the exchange differently, the way we should have in the first place. We met up in the bathroom in stalls next to each other and simply exchanged the shirts above the stall walls. The 3X fit me much better, still a little too big, but I was happy with it. I didn't understand why everyone wanted a button down shirt. I actually didn't like them. Because of my allergy to nickel, the metal snaps caused me to have a rash were they touched my skin.

I was starting to notice at that time that all of the clothes issued to me at intake were loose, which could only mean one thing…I was losing weight and I wasn't even dieting. A few days later, I had an appointment with the P.A. and I had lost twenty pounds! It was the easiest weight loss I had ever experienced. I thanked God, because I knew that He was helping me and surely had blessed me. It didn't hurt that I had skipped a few meals because I was too exhausted to walk to the chow hall and the food was nasty. Without any seasoning, it was bland, I reasoned that the food here was like the food they served in nursing homes. I got to thinking, how much weight could I lose?

CHAPTER 7

The Crown Prince Speaks

But as for me, my prayer is to you, O Lord, in the acceptable time; O God, in the multitude of your mercy, hear me in the truth of Your salvation. Deliver me out of the mire and let me not sink; let me be delivered from those who hate me and out of the deep waters. Let not the floodwater overflow me, nor let the deep swallow me up; and let not the pit shut it's mouth on me.
- Psalm 69:13-15

I wasn't prepared for this part of my journey and I certainly wasn't prepared for all of the he/she activity. I have known a few lesbians and homosexuals, but what goes on behind the barbed wire is an abomination, pure and simple. The women that are living this lifestyle here are just deviants, love has nothing to do with it. It is obvious that it is mostly about domination and submissive perversions and there is nothing covert about it. Sexual gratification is at the top of the list and there is no shame associated with this behavior.

I understood the loneliness of imprisonment, however, being "Gay for the stay" wasn't going to happen for me. The mass number of them is obvious, they were everywhere on the campus, even the back rows of the Church services. The pastor was appalled and now the back rows are taped off so that everyone has to sit up front. It is sickening behavior and the worst part of it is, I couldn't get away from it. All of the different cells that I was housed in, had at least one in it. The cell I spent the most time in was a four bed room and I was the only non-partaker of this perversion. The sexual activity of these women was off the chain.

We were only allowed out of our cells at limited times to use the restroom, go to common areas or go to the "Big" yard for recreation. On one of my trips to the restroom, I walked by the stalls, looking for an open one, and unbelievable, in the last stall there were two inmates having sex and it was clear they didn't care who knew or could hear them. I was speechless. I must have looked shocked, there were a couple of other inmates standing around the corner and when they saw me, they just laughed. It finally occurred to me that they were the lookouts, watching the C.O.'s at the base, right across from the restroom. They were making sure that the "couple" would have time to carry on and not get caught. I don't know if I blushed or not, my cheeks felt warm, and I definitely wasn't going to go near that last stall.

I was so out of my element and definitely out of my comfort zone. My frustration was mounting and all I wanted to do was to stay in my cell and sleep and read my Bible and have my conversations with God. That time alone with the Creator was precious, it was the only thing that was real, truthful and calming. I needed to have something to hold on to and God was definitely holding my hand. I needed that if I wasn't going to be swallowed up by this place.

Well, well, well, the day finally arrived, my bunkie was called down to the base and when she came back, she started packing, she was finally going over to the general population. She had told me earlier that she didn't care which unit she would be assigned to with one exception, Calhoun. Calhoun was the unit that youngest women, 21 and under were housed. We all had heard stories of how it was "off the chain," for being loud, drug use and no control over their actions. I was so glad that I wouldn't be assigned to that unit. She was turning 22 soon and was adamant she didn't want to go there.

I had lived long enough that it often seemed like that those things you didn't want to happen, happened and it was the way it was going down this time too. My bunkie found out she was going to Calhoun. I found it quite humorous considering she had asked the ARUS for a new bunkie closer to her age. We have all heard "Be careful for what you ask for, you might just get it." She was going to be surrounded by them twenty-four seven.

There was always a buzz on the floor when people were being moved out, that meant that new people would be moved in. The inmate across the hall that had traded that shirt with me, told me that a gal from her hometown was waiting to be moved up. She was currently down on the A wing, the quarantine wing and maybe I would be lucky and have her assigned to my cell. She said the young woman was genuine, mature beyond her years, calm and best of all, a Christian. I thought to myself that would be a blessing indeed!

Big blessings come in beautiful packages, my new bunkie was indeed the woman that I had heard about. I had no doubt that God had once again showed His mercy and grace on me. I learned that she too had been praying to God for a good bunkie. She went on to say that she was very fearful about moving upstairs and I could relate. I thought back to that time, not so long ago, waiting to be moved upstairs. It was a time full of anxiety and fear. I remember smiling to myself knowing that God had answered both of our prayers and I also knew that He was smiling, happy for both of us knowing that He had put two believers together.

I found that my spirit was instantly lifted with the knowledge that my new bunkie desired God's Word as much as I did. She was trying to live in the Light in that dark place, behind the barbed wire.

When my new bunkie found out I was writing about my experience in prison, she was intrigued. She had quite a story of her own. Amazingly, she had a sister there at the same time serving a five year sentence for a third offense D.U.I. and this was actually her second time in prison. I later met her sister and she was a lovely woman. It still amazes me how so many of us, decent human beings were trying to bury our childhoods with drugs, alcohol and of course my choice of "drugs" was/is food. That however, is a topic for another time and book.

My new bunkie was more beautiful on the inside than even her outside beauty. Her beauty radiates from within and I believe it was God radiating out of her. She was there for the poor choices she made in friends and using drugs. I hope and pray that her time at W.H.V. was spent wisely and she will never return to either drugs or prison. It was hard to believe that she was the same age as my previous bunkie, she was so much more mature.

Out of the blue, I was called down to the base and informed that I had an attorney visit and to dress in my state blues and return to the base for further instructions. I wondered if it was the attorney that represented me for this case or was it the appeals attorney that I requested and if it was the latter, that was sure fast.

As I approached the base, I saw the C.O. giving me the once over and her eyes stopped on my head. She asked me if I had contraband in my hair. I said no and she pointed to my headband made up of pony tail rubber bands looped together. I took it off and she proceeded to throw them in the trash can. Alone, the pony tail bands weren't contraband, however, when looped together they were, another lesson learned.

I was escorted over to the east side of the general population area to the visitor's center. Once there, after waiting in line, I was led to a room where another officer had me strip down and I was searched, for what I didn't have a clue. By this time, I actually had become numb to the entire process of stripping down or being patted down. I didn't feel I had the luxury to be modest or embarrassed. After re-dressing, I was led to another room to wait for my visitor.

I had time to look around and see inmates interacting with their family and friends or those still waiting to be reunited, staring into space. It was a cathedral ceiling and every noise was amplified. The saddest thing to watch were the new mothers, those that gave birth to their babies while in prison, having them taken away after two days, now visiting with the infants and toddlers only to find that the children did not know them and actually were very resistant to being held by their birth mother. How sad it was, I thought back to my own son and I remembered that he was a year old before I even left him with his father. I was so attached to him and I knew that to be separated from him would have killed me. Those poor mothers.

I was finally ordered to go to the small room off of the main room. I sat down in one of the two chairs provided with a table in between them both. A stranger came into the room, didn't shut the door for privacy and sat down. He introduced himself as the partner of the attorney that had been assigned to my appeals case. He said he was there visiting other inmates and wanted to meet me. Even though I knew it was a possibility that the appeals attorney might be the visitor, I was still stunned, I had only sent the paperwork in two weeks earlier. I had been told by the unreliable "inmate.com" that it usually took about six weeks to be contacted.

The first thing that he said was that they were going to take my case and he was there to get additional information. After I had answered all of his questions, he said my case was like an apple, so different from the usual cases that were assigned to their office. It would be like comparing apples to oranges. Securities violations were usually handled by the federal not state government. He didn't elaborate and I was still slow in thinking, brain dead and never asked him what he meant by that statement. He told me to be patient, that they were going to have to research security law cases and with that, stood up and left the room. He left quickly and gave me the impression that he didn't want to shake my hand or come close to me.

So, once again, "inmate.com" was wrong on another matter. I was told that visitors usually bought snacks and drinks from the vending machines out in the main room for the inmate they were visiting. What a disappointment! I had let my guard down and hoped that the information was correct, after all, this visit was during dinner time and I would miss my meal. As I sat in the main room waiting to be led back to the inspection room, I realized that in lieu of food, he had brought me good news and God knew that I needed good news even more than food. After being stripped searched again, I was escorted back to Unit 9 and there was a dinner tray waiting for me. It was cold, but it was food.

It was another sleepless night. I tossed and turned and my mind just wouldn't shut down. I kept going over and over the attorney's visit. What did he mean about comparing apples to oranges? What did they see in my case file that stood out, what was it they found that would cause them to believe that an appeal was necessary, let alone winnable?

I was clueless, I thought I had paid for a good attorney to fight my battles, the more I thought about it, my BIGGEST mistake was actually in not taking this whole mess to God. I never asked Him at any time during this process to help me. Was it a matter of trust? Sad to say, it was just a matter of not living a life with God as the main focus. I was living and leading a life all about me. It wasn't until after I got to prison that I had turned it all over to Him. I was angry at myself for not turning it over to Him from the very first, the outcome, might have been very different, or not. It was at this point that I started to think that God might want me to be there. But, what could be His reason? I knew that God always turned the negative into a positive, that out of this darkness, a light would be seen. I started to thank Him in my prayers for allowing me to be incarcerated and that I would try to be patient and asked for strength to get through this. It was only with this turn of my prayers that I started to feel any safety and peace. I just needed to stay in the moment, looking ahead was still full of anxiety.

I had been skipping a lot of meals, with no appetite or energy to make it to the chow hall. What concerned me was that in general population, the chow hall would be in a separate building, not like the in-house chow hall here. The distance from the housing unit would depend on which unit I would be assigned to. There were units close and there were units a bit of a distance. I really didn't have a sense of how the general population was laid out. Of course, I could go to "inmate.com" and we know how that usually turned out.

I just wanted to do my time, paying my debt to society and go home and try to rebuild a life for myself. That was something that I couldn't spend too much time pondering. The future was definitely scary and I just couldn't go there. I had to stay focused on the present and that present meant, where I was going to be housed, that would make all of the difference on how I was going to live day to day making it to the end of my sentence.

From what I had gathered, general population was divided into two sides. The west side and east side. The first timers, non-violent, and shorter sentences were usually housed on the east side. Because of the huge overcrowding, it appeared that people were being put wherever a bed was available, thereby mixing different levels of inmates. I was also told that because I had a lower bunk detail, it could take longer to be sent over.

My bunkie and I were getting along very well. What a difference it made in getting through the day. We got to talk about God and we knew that each of us were really interested in the love of our Father. Wow. I knew then as I know now that God had sent her to me when I needed an angel to share the gift of His love.

I finally received a letter from my son, the Crown Prince. I was so relieved and overjoyed that I forgot that I was angry that I had not heard from him. As he explained in the letter, the postcards he had written to me and sent to the county jail were sent back, not forwarded to me. He had enclosed them in his letter, they had the information I needed, so I finally had his address and phone number. It just so happened that it was my phone day and I wanted to call him. It felt so good to know we finally were connecting.

I was so anxious about not having money to purchase items for the next store. I also wanted to encourage him to go to the websites that could give him valuable information about how to support his family member in prison. It would be a huge step in the right direction, finally. Progress was being made.

Later that day, my joy turned into anxiety as I was trying to establish the phone service. I had trouble hearing the automated operator give the instructions and my anxiety did not help. The phones were located in the hallway and the echo of the noise made it nearly impossible for me to hear. Phone usage was only permitted during our hall's recreation period, so the hall was even noisier than usual.

As I dialed my son's phone number, I was shaking, this was my first connection to the world and to the person who meant the most to me. It was the only voice that could make me cry and it was the only voice I wanted to hear. What if he didn't answer? Would it go to voice mail, using my one free minute? I told myself to just breathe. I knew that we would only have this one minute unless he put money on his phone so we could talk longer. I heard his voice say hello and the automated operator told him who the call was from and gave him instructions on how to put money on his phone for further conversation after the one free minute. I couldn't tell if he had or not, I was too excited to talk and get everything I had to say said in those sixty seconds.

My heart melted at "Hello mom." After telling him I loved him, I immediately asked why he hadn't put money on my account, after all, he had my checking account for the funds. I needed hygiene products, postage, food, etc. I asked why didn't he send the quarterly box? He was clueless, actually he had no idea what I was talking about. I was stunned. He went on to say that he had been very busy at work and in addition to all of the extra duties of taking care of my "stuff." In my impatience, I snapped and I remember saying, "Crack heads can figure out how to put money on their phones and how to add money to their woman's account on jpay and use the email system, why couldn't he? Just at that moment, the automated operator interrupted saying the minute was up and to add minutes to his phone he needed to have his credit card available. I was so upset, I wasn't hearing well and so baffled by his answers, I just hung up on him...fine. I decided that I would just find someone else less busy and more dedicated to my needs while I was here. To say I was incensed would have been an understatement of all time.

I went back to my cell to calm down and reflect on what had just happened. I was just stunned, at a loss for words when my bunkie asked me how it went. I laid down on my bunk and didn't say a word. Laying there, feeling the tears roll down my face, numbing out so that the pain would just go away. All I could think about was getting out of there and not just the prison, but life itself. I knew that suicide was a sin, thou shalt not kill, and that included self, but since I was going to escape out of the prison that had to be the only way out. I told God, I was sorry, but the pain had to stop, I hoped that He would forgive me, but this was going to be the path I was going to take. In prison, there are two ways to commit suicide, by hanging or an overdose. Since I had never did drugs, I would have to find a place to hang myself. The prison had taken precautions in making it difficult to find anywhere to hang. It became my obsession, looking for places and the means to die by. I didn't tell anyone because even the hint of what I was thinking could have me sent to segregation and I wasn't going to let that happen or stop me. The day after the phone debacle, at recreation time, I checked the jpay system and actually had a couple of messages from friends that had figured out how to put money on the account and message me. In addition to them, the Crown Prince had finally figured it out too! I was shocked! Of course, I opened his mail first and he told me he would try to figure everything out and that with his busy schedule, he wouldn't be able to take my calls, so he hadn't put money on his phone for calls from me. So…there it was, like it or not.

I have had a lot of abandonment issues in my life and this was just one more in a long line. In all reality, God has been the only one who has never abandoned me and has always loved me, unconditionally. It was at times like these that I ran to Him and could actually "feel" His loving arms, He is my refuge in times of darkness. He had blessed me with not only His love but His understanding and it was my greatest desire to know Him more fully. I reminded Him that I had asked for just that when I was in the intake cell.

One good thing to say about prison, I would have time without noise and distractions from the outside world and would be able to be still and focus on Him. In my passion to know Him intimately, I would have to trust Him and believe that He knew what was best. That would mean letting Him make decisions for me and me following. I still smile at that. Me, a follower? I had a hard time dancing, being the follower, even there, I wanted to lead. Trust was something I was going to have to work on.

I had always been a planner, a leader and very driven to do and get what I wanted. In fact, there are some that could have called me a control diva. I had always felt "blessed" that I could manage so well on my own. Of course, that was the illusion, the illusion of control helped me feel safe, which was the biggest illusion, the big lie.

CHAPTER 8

The Wailing

I cried unto God with my voice, even unto God with my voice and He gave ear unto me. In the day of trouble I sought the Lord: my sore ran in the night, and ceased not: My soul refused to be comforted. I remembered God, and was troubled: I complained, and my spirit was overwhelmed. Thou holdest mine eyes waking: I am so troubled that I cannot speak.
- **Psalm 77:1-4**

I don't know if I will ever be able to find the right words to convey what happened that night. Life in prison is real and often times raw, raw to the core.

That night I didn't go to chow, just one of the many nights my energy was gone and my body ached and it was one of the few times I could be alone with the solitude and quiet. I felt so suffocated by being constantly surrounded by people and their noise. It wasn't that my bunkie was loud, I just had the need to be by myself, alone with my thoughts, alone with God to re-energize. My entire lifetime had been drained of my life's energy by people and noise. It is strange, but I love public speaking, it is a rush, however, as soon as I am done, I am drained and need to find a place of solitude to enjoy the peace and quiet...to rejuvenate.

I must have fallen asleep shortly after most of the inmates on the wing had gone downstairs to the mess hall. I awoke to someone screaming to a C.O. "…she did it, she did it, she finally did it!" It took me a few moments to realize I wasn't dreaming and to find clarity. I got up from the bed and went to the cell door that my bunkie had left ajar. I peeked out of the doorway towards the front of the hall and saw a C.O. running to an inmate's cell which was located towards the front of the hall. She was trying to open the door using her body like a battling ram. The door wasn't budging an inch with all of her efforts and strength. What chilled me to the bone was the agonizing sound of her voice, wailing over and over, "Oh..." It was a cry of such anguish, compassion, frustration and a sense of complete devastation. She was using her walkie-talkie to call for backup and as she was talking, she turned and saw me standing at my door. I must have looked puzzled and she yelled at me to go back into the cell and shut the door. There were other voices talking back and forth, so I knew that there were others still up on the floor. As it turned out, the three inmates were all friends of the inmate in trouble. It occurred to me in that moment that they all knew what was behind that barricaded door and in fact, so did the C.O.

I stepped back from the doorway, just out of sight and listened to what was happening. There were footsteps rapidly coming up the stairs and shouting as the C.O. continued to wail. I peeked out and saw three other C.O.'s trying to open the door. I didn't know what the inmate had done to barricade the door, but whatever she did, she did a great job. It was obvious to me that she didn't want to be found. Stepping back in the cell, close to the open door, I heard gasps as the door was finally breached. Through all of the grunting and yelling, I heard the C.O. still wailing "Oh ….."

I heard the officers discussing what was inside, their voices showing no emotion, still working to resolve the situation. Evidently, the inmate was naked, on the floor with numerous cuts to her arms. I remembered that this inmate was not new to cutting, the scars were all over her arms, legs and face. She must have swallowed whatever she had used to slice her arms. Someone yelled down to the base for a big plastic sheet, they were going to pull her out of her cell, obviously wanting as little movement to her until they could assess the situation. I have to tell you, at that moment all I could think of was the "Keystone Kops," they didn't know what they were doing. Hadn't they ever rehearsed what to do in emergency situations like this? I was so appalled! The inmate was unconscious, she was not responding to them repeatedly calling her name.

As I was listening, I was in disbelief with what I was hearing. It was unbelievable, the staff were so ill prepared for this, making recovery up as they went. It was obvious that they were at a loss, I could hear it the voice of the officer that finally asked "Should we call for the E.M.T.'s?" I gasped as I heard "Should we apply a tourniquet?" I think that it was at this time that I turned from total unbelief to anger. Anger that the E.M.T.'s weren't called first thing, anger that the staff were so incompetent, I was angry at the inmate for doing this!

In my previous life in the work world, most of the companies had training for the worst case scenarios in that area of business. They were drilled over and over so that in a state of emergency, everyone knew what their roll was and what they were supposed to do for a positive outcome. I didn't have a good feeling about this, it was patently obvious that this crew was clueless. It was also very clear that MDOC had not trained the staff and that made me really angry. When I think about it now, I am sure that this wasn't the first time something like this had happened and I am sure it wouldn't be the last.

I had to sit down on my bunk, I was starting to shake and suddenly lost all of my energy. I noticed that I was rocking, something that as a child I did to self-comfort. The sobbing started and I started asking the Angels of Light to surround the inmate and praying to God to take care of her and give the staff wisdom to do what had to be done. Still rocking, I looked up from my praying to see an officer watching me. She asked if I was okay? I nodded no and she just closed the door I had left ajar. I heard her making her way down the hallway, stopping at the cell doors that were also ajar, asking if they were okay and shutting the doors. When she got to the cell door right across from the activity in the hall, she asked if they saw anything. It struck me as odd that she didn't ask them if they knew what had happened or if they knew that it was going to happen. It was strange that she didn't ask more questions, it was as if she didn't really want to know.

Earlier in the day, I had observed this inmate crying and apparently very upset and I asked her if she was okay? She shook her head, no...she had just learned that her brother had O.D.'d and she didn't know if he was going to pull through. She wasn't alone, she was with another inmate, the inmate that helped me with my duffel bag the day I was moved up on the floor, and they were sitting very close to the fence. I didn't think anything about that at the time. It was a sunny day and I thought she needed someone to talk things over with. What I failed to remember at that time, was that no one was allowed just to loiter in the front yard of the Unit. It was also forbidden to stand, let alone sit next to the fence. On the other side of the fence there were rolls of coiled barb wire. Later when I inspected the coils, I noticed missing barbs, in fact, quite a few of them and I learned that was exactly what she did, using the broken off barbs to cut herself then swallow the blades. How she did it with that area surrounded with cameras, I couldn't imagine. The only explanation was that no one was watching the monitors, which wasn't unusual.

To make matters worse, I learned that earlier that day, she had gone down to the base and informed the officer on duty what she had learned about her brother and felt that she might harm herself, thus needing to be taken to "bam-bam." "Bam-bam" is where inmates are taken to a cell, stripped of their clothing, only able to wear a quilted gown, with a bed with only a mattress and a quilted cover. They are observed 24 hours a day with no privacy. It is not a place that you want to be housed in unless you are in dire straits, either protecting you from yourself or someone else. This inmate knew what it entailed, she had been there many times before. I heard that she was told to go back to her cell and rest. Given her history, that didn't make any sense to me.

If that is true and I had no reason to doubt that it was, why did it have to happen this way? If the MDOC staff were aware of even the slightest possibility that she would harm herself, why weren't precautions taken? Her face and body were scarred from earlier attempts when she had been incarcerated before. She was seeing a psychiatrist and psychologist, on medication, all of which they were aware of. It is my opinion that MDOC was negligent in how this all played out.

She had to be dragged and carried out that night on a plastic bag, down the hallway and steps, all the way out to MDOC's ambulance, not even Ypsilanti's Emergency Ambulance. Why wasn't she taken to the hospital? Why was she taken only to the prison's medical center? I remember getting angrier and angrier the more I thought about it, obviously MDOC didn't want this to be made public.

This wasn't the first time while I was there and wouldn't be the last time that a tragedy would be kept from being made public. By keeping everything "in house," they avoided questions and some of those questions they had no answer for. They also avoided lawsuits and outrage by the public at large, at least I had hoped that the public cared.

I was haunted by the C.O.'s sorrowful wailing and how eerie it was in the silence after she was taken out. There were no sirens, only the flashing of the vehicle's lights coming in through the cell windows. Silence in prison is rare and always meant that something had happened.

The inmates in Unit 9, D wing were finally allowed back to their cells after the unit porters cleaned up. They had been detained in the chow hall during the event and when my bunkie came in, she immediately started asking me questions, and she knew that I had been up on the floor during the whole mess. She told me that after they were locked in the cafeteria, the rumors started, it seemed there were many people who knew just how despondent she had been.

I shared with her what I had heard and what I had seen. We prayed for her, the staff and all of the inmates there. It was unspoken, but I know we both were thinking about what would happen if either one of us should find ourselves in trouble, that more than likely it would be kept quiet or at best a story with as little information as possible given to our families. Felon's lives, don't matter. It was a rough night trying to find sleep to dull the pain.

The next morning, standing in line for morning medications, I stood behind the inmate's "ex-wife." They had met and "married" when they were here before. She was the same inmate who had screamed for the C.O. the night before. I could feel my anger growing moment by moment, knowing that anger in prison was not a good thing. I finally couldn't contain myself and leaned forward and asked, "You knew what she was going to do, didn't you?" She replied, "Yes, but I didn't think she would go that far or it would be that bad." As she talked to me, she couldn't look me in the eye and with each word she spoke, my anger grew. I had to ask God to help me or I would make a choice that wouldn't be good. I asked her if she had heard whether or not she had made it or not and her reply was, "I don't know." It was a good thing that it was her turn to go in and get her medications and even a greater thing that she was being released later that morning.

She had explained to me that the parole board had determined that her parole violation did not warrant extra time behind bars, she was going home, she was going to be free.

Even now, after being out of prison, I am haunted by that night, I can still hear that C.O.'s wailing and the feeling that I didn't matter, that my life could have ended and no one would even care. I know that isn't true, however, that was my reality.

I kept the C.O. in my prayers and wanted to write her a note of compassion for what she had seen, but that would be forbidden, after all, to show any compassion in prison is a sign of weakness. While I will forever be haunted by what I heard, she will be haunted by what she was able to see that I didn't.

What is shocking is that at about the same time that the incident happened, we heard that another inmate had been successful in killing herself after asking to go to Bam-bam. When something like this happens, the prison makes sure that if or when it is reported on the news that those stations are blocked so that the inmates can't learn anything about it. In fact, when the local newspapers report the incidents, they too are banned. It wasn't until I was doing research for this book that I found out what actually happened to the dead inmate.

You can read the article at The Detroit Free Press, Published 10:56 p.m. ET Feb. 28, 2017 by Paul Egan in regards to Women's Huron Valley Correctional Facility or: https://www.freep.com/story/news/local/michigan/2017/02/28/lawsuit-filed-over-suicide-inmate-michigans-only-womens-prison/98534254/

CHAPTER 9

Moving On Up To
The East Side

Hear me, O Lord, for Your Lovingkindness is good, turn to me according to the multitude of Your tender mercies. And do not hide Your face from Your servant, for I am in trouble; hear me speedily. Draw near my soul, and redeem it; deliver me because of my enemies.

You know my reproach, my shame, and my dishonor; my adversaries are all before You. Reproach has broken my heart, and I am full of heaviness; I looked for someone to take pity, but there was none; and for comforters, but I found none.
- Psalm 69:16-20

In order to find some semblance of normalcy, whatever that was, after the tragedy that night, my bunkie and I had a day at the spa. While we were housed in Unit 9, we weren't allowed to have nail clippers, once we were moved over to the general population, we could order them on the store. Nail files are strictly forbidden anywhere on the grounds. I had

50

discovered the perfect nail "file" and wanted to share it with my cellmate. My nails had really grown and needed to be maintained and looking at hers, they did too.

Once I told her we needed a little R&R at the spa, I asked her to join me sitting on the floor. I had discovered that the cement floor was perfect for filing my nails! So, we sat there and filed and shaped our nails and talked like we were at the spa. I tried to do my toe nails, however, I wasn't at all flexible enough to bend my legs into a position that I could manage that. Of course, "Ms. Yoga" herself managed to do her toes. It is strange how something so normal but not normal could brighten our day. Who knew that filing nails on a cement floor could be so fun! We were able to laugh and just for a few minutes forget that we were in prison, in a cell with a cement floor and bars on the window.

Of course, in Unit 9 we were not allowed to have tweezers. My eyebrows stayed in pretty good shape, having thinned out with age, however, for every eyebrow lash, I had one hair growing on my chin and they had to be pulled out. She had learned to thread while she was in jail waiting to be sent to prison. She threaded my chin/neck area and my upper lip and eyebrows and after that went to work on herself.

I had come to look for and found blessings in the smallest things. I was glad that we had that evening together, because the following day I was called to move over to the east side.

I had been in Unit 9, RGC for 72 days. At that time, I had been on the D wing longer than anyone there with exception of the P.V. that had helped with finding a used Bible for me, she was still waiting for a decision from the parole board in regards to her parole violation. She had been in the unit almost 6 months.

When the officer called FAHER, I knew my time had finally come, it was finally my turn and so did everyone on the wing. As I walked down the hall, down the stairs and onto the base, I was instructed to pack-up, that I would be moving to Unit HA-27D. I had no idea which unit that was, but I knew that God knew and was He was handling everything. Even with that trust, my anxiety was skyrocketing. My biggest fear was being moved to a 10 or 16 bed cell and being far from the chow hall.

As I walked back upstairs and down the hall, almost everyone was in their cell door, asking where I was going? It was pretty much the same ritual when someone finally had their turn to move out. It meant that after someone left, they would be closer to their turn.

To prepare for the anxiety that I knew would come once I had my orders to pack-up, I actually had done a little pre-packing. I packed up the Outlander books that my dear friend Ingrid had sent me, they were so heavy. I added a few other things that I thought I would not be needing in the near future and stuffed the duffel bag into my locker. I knew that it was breaking a rule that nothing was to be in our duffel bags.

I was sad that I was leaving my beautiful bunkie behind, but I knew that she would be sent to the east side as well and probably to Calhoun with the other younger inmates.

After packing the duffel bag to its capacity, I dragged it down the hall and when I finally reached the stairs, I turned and faced the inmates in their cell doors and waved and told them to be kind to each other. With that, I turned around to descend the stairs when the unit rep. came forward from her cell and asked if she could carry my bag for me. Of course I said yes and thanked her and God for sending me an angel at my hour of need. It was another of the blessings that I was receiving on a daily basis.

There were three of us that moved over that day, one for the west side and two for the east side. It was the second day of June and was already hot and very humid with light rain off and on all day. All of our bags, T.V.'s and other bags were put on a cart used for moving inmates to their new quarters. It was heavy and the wheels didn't always want to go forward, but I took my turn pulling the cart. I was the last one to be dropped off, which wasn't good considering that my strength was all but gone. I would have preferred being dropped off first.

Harrison had two wings, side A and side B. I had been assigned to side A which I found out was the wing dedicated to pregnant inmates. It was smaller than most units and yes, it was the farthest from the chow hall and it turned out that it was the farthest from everything else as well, with the exception being the Medical Center and Visitors Center. As to my cell, you probably guessed it, I was assigned to a ten bed cell. It had originally been the T.V. room, but because of the overcrowding it was converted into housing. The T.V. was added to the day room with the library, game tables, kitchenette and kiosks. The combination of the two didn't mix well. The front of the room had inmates watching the T.V. and reading books while everyone else was talking, cooking, and playing games in the back of the room. It was seldom harmonious and to make matters worse, only 38 people were allowed in the room and there were 62 beds in the facility. It was always a challenge to find a seat. The rule was that there wasn't to be anyone standing, only sitting.

After sitting in the day room, waiting for the paperwork to go through before I went to my new cell I was called to go on a tour of the unit by the unit's representative. Everything looked clean and neat and I could tell an attempt was made at one time to have a theme of under the sea décor. My cell was right behind the officer's base. When I walked in, the enormity of the room stunned me. After being in a two person cell, this was so spacious, I definitely wasn't going to get claustrophobia.

Everyone introduced themselves, they seemed pretty laid back. They said due to the size of the room, there was a lot of coming and going because not everyone liked a ten bed room. They seemed to like the size of the room and having nine other cellmates didn't bother them. There were a few desks that we could play cards on and hang out. After I unpacked and made up my bed, I laid down and tried to zone out. I needed time to relax and re-group, not being someone who did well with changes.

Later in the day, I was given the "rules" of the cell. Everyone had an assigned day to clean and my assigned day was Wednesday. That would consist of sweeping, mopping, and disinfecting the common areas of the cell. I took the day that the last person in the cell had. Because there were only seven days to the week and we had ten people, I was told that those inmates that had been in the cell the longest, got knocked out of the rotation. The cell lights Sunday through Thursday were turned off at eleven and Friday and Saturday they could stay on until midnight. That everyone would try to be considerate in the morning because half of the room liked to sleep in, missing breakfast. I knew that I would be among that group.

One of the most memorable things to happen on that day occurred while I was in the day room. An inmate, that looked about twenty-five, had lots of tattoos, moved in front of me, squatted and shook her butt which moved like jello. I was stunned, however, I sat there motionless while everyone in the room was roaring with laughter. She went on to ask me if I could do that and I told her no, that I was too old to be twerking. Everyone laughed again and then went back to what they were doing. That was my introduction and welcoming to the unit. When I got back to the cell, I told my bunkies about it and they laughed and said that she twerked a lot.

The walk to the chow hall seemed to go on forever and due to the overcrowding the line was long. Standing was not easy at that time and to make matters worse, people saved places for their friends which only extended the standing time. The Medical Center was very close and the line was long for that too.

I had an appointment with the dietician at the Medical Center, she weighed me and in the three months I had been there, I had lost thirty pounds. I had notice that my clothes were getting very loose, but I hadn't been dieting so I figured God was still helping me and the pounds were just melting off of me. She asked me how I was doing that, considering that the average inmate gained thirty-five pounds the first year. I told her that I was missing a lot of meals, it was too long of a walk to the chow hall because of a lack of energy and the arthritic pain that I felt afterwards. I think that it was a God-thing. I really wasn't hungry and the food wasn't that appetizing or even nutritious, despite what the dietician said. Of course, she lectured me about missing meals and gave me some brochures about dieting with exercise. There was a whole page dedicated to exercises that could be done in the cell.

Since I hadn't signed up to see her, I asked her what made her call me out? She reminded me that when I filled out the questionnaire at intake, I had indicated that I wanted to lose weight as my number one goal for my time spent there. I was impressed that someone had actually read it. As I walked back to my unit, which wasn't very far, I remember smiling thinking I definitely was going to be in better physical shape than when I came in.

There were no dull moments and that might seem odd considering that each day we all had a routine to follow. What made it different is that we all were pieces to be moved on the MDOC board game that none of us asked to play, however, we definitely were in "prison." Each morning we received an itinerary of our day's scheduled activities. Most of the activities were assigned to us by MDOC and those activities that we had signed up for in unit 9 were mostly filled up and there were long waiting lists for. That itinerary was called a detail. Each of us had better be at the location specified and the time specified or we might be considered out of place with various punishments for that. We were told it was for our security and for MDOC to be able to monitor our whereabouts at any given time.

When you have an activity, you take your detail up to the base and have the officer sign you out and when you return, you are supposed to be signed back in, however, that rarely happened, it was one of the areas that the staff was very lax in. Signing up for an activity was called "Kiting" and put you on the list for the activities you might like to do. I had signed up for yoga and was so excited the day that I looked at my detail and saw that it had been scheduled. That excitement didn't last long, after a long walk to the field house where the class was led by a yoga instructor, a fellow inmate, I was exhausted. I had no idea that I was so out of shape! It seemed all of my muscles were tight and ached if they thought they were going to be used or abused. So, I couldn't bend and my balance had left me years ago. My weight definitely added to the problem, making yoga something I wasn't able to do at that time. I remember thinking to myself that hopefully, I would be able to do it at a later time, maybe with more weight loss I could do it. So, for the time being, I was going to give it up. If you miss more than three classes in a row, you are taken off of the rotation and that is exactly what I did. I would "kite" for it later and make sure that I had appropriate shoes and pants. I had to remind myself that at this stage, I was like the butterfly in the cocoon and in a couple of years, I would emerge to be transformed in the beautiful butterfly that I was destined to be.

Most of my cell mates liked to stay busy, they said it made the time go by faster. For me, it caused a lot of anxiety. For my entire stay, every morning when I looked at my detail, I had anxiety and the only thing that brought it down was when nothing other than my med. lines were scheduled. I would wake up early to look at it and then go back to bed and relax and get a little more sleep. Our beds had to be made by 8 a.m. and we had to be fully dressed, so I made my bed and slept on top of it. Time never seemed to go slow for me. I knew that I had things that I wanted to accomplish, my weight, get a handle on my health issues and of course, my favorite, my time with God, getting to know Him better through His word.

One of my cellmates was a woman close to my age and we bonded. We were the two "old women" in the cell and enjoyed each other's company. She wasn't in the cell very often, she stayed busy going to school in building trades and worked clear across the campus at the administrative building as a cleaning woman. I found her to be a kind, loving, compassionate woman, I found her to be real, something that was hard to find. She wasn't loud and on her day off, she liked to sleep in like I did. She had been in the room the longest and was no longer in the cleaning rotation. It seemed like the ten bed cell was like a revolving door, in just a short time that I was there, five women had come in and transferred out.

Every day, the biggest topic of conversation was the overcrowding and how it really impacted our daily lives as well as the staff. I prayed every day for patience, the lines were so long for chow, med. lines, showers and the toilets. The increase in the numbers didn't mean that more showers and toilets were installed.

I had time to give the overcrowding some thought. What was happening that women were being incarcerated at a record's pace? There had to be something that was going on that the numbers had increased and were still increasing. I actually came to the conclusion that there might be two or three reasons. Number one, so many of the women here, were here for drug offenses and everything related to that. I had never seen so many woman with their teeth rotted out or completely missing. I was told that an inmate had to be there for two years before dentures would be made for her. The drugs of choice seemed to be heroin or meth. Having never used drugs, I was so clueless to the drug culture. It seemed to me that if someone was an addict, that treatment would be the first choice. Many of the women told me the judges that sentenced them said they wish there was a place for them to receive treatment, but there weren't enough facilities and many of the women had been in treatment before and weren't given the chance to go again.

Number two, it was my opinion that the judicial system in Michigan had become political. The administration at that time was pro keeping inmates in prison and not letting them out for "good time." The political machine had did a great job of fear mongering the public that they were not safe if felons got out for good behavior. They often cited the felons that got out of prison and then committed a violent crime. Statistically that wasn't the norm, however, it was effective in keeping the citizens in line with no early releases. In 1998, the dissolution of "good time" was on the ballot and voted in. I couldn't remember if I voted for it or not, but there was a good chance that I too had voted for the amendment. There were actually people that spoke out against it, citing that overcrowding would ensue and would cost the tax payers much more. The cost to the public was about $35,000 a year per inmate and if the inmate was using the medical system, it was estimated to be at $42,000 per year.

What I found amusing was that the 82 counties of Michigan all endorsed "good time" at their county jails and there wasn't a public outcry about that.

Just like the states that use the death penalty as a deterrent, Michigan uses "good time" as a deterrent. The problem is that the statistics didn't support the theory. When we were able to get our hands on a current newspaper, there were quite a few editorials about the over-crowing and that "good time" should be brought back, like the surrounding states. I was like most tax payers in that if something didn't affect me personally, I wasn't going to give it much thought. This is food for thought, if inmates thought that good behavior was synonymous with getting out of incarceration early, would that be a good thing?

The final piece that did affect me, was the judicial system sending non-violent offenders to prison for longer sentences. I had always been taught that people that went to prison were a danger to society. I met plenty of women that definitely were not a danger or threat to society. There had to be other ways to punish offenders without putting them into prison. The age old question still exists, do we want to punish the prisoner or rehabilitate the prisoner.

CHAPTER 10

Finding My J.O.B.

To You, O Lord, I lift up my soul. O my God, I trust in You;
let me not be ashamed; let not mine enemies triumph over me.
Indeed, let no one who waits on You be ashamed; let those be
ashamed who deal treacherously with cause.
- **Psalm 25:1-3**

I had blocked time out of each day to write this book. I made a cup of coffee and sat in the cell at one of the tables that I used as my desk and wrote for about an hour each day. Everyone knew what I was doing, so they pretty much left me alone. I let everyone know that I was going to my J.O.B. and would be unavailable for about an hour.

I asked my best friend Jan, to send me a copy of my beloved book, Jesus Calling by Sarah Young. My Aunt Roberta had given me a copy a few years ago and I felt that God was talking to me through each page and I missed that. My morning ritual with God consisted of reading Our Daily Bread, Jesus Calling and my Bible. I noticed that I was spending more and more time in the Word which brought me not only comfort, but it was helping me with my concentration. I could feel God blessing me with His Grace and Love.

I asked God to lead me, what did He want me to do while I was in prison? It actually didn't take long before I heard the answer, helping people, even in prison was my J.O.B. in addition to writing the book. I have always had the sense that God would use me, I just never gave it any thought that it might be in the middle of prison. So, I decided to put together a seminar and make it available to the entire prison. It was a daunting task, while I knew the material, my memory was still like Swiss cheese. God was going to have to lead me on this, I needed His strength and support. I was excited, yet at the same time wondered if I really could do it.

I met with the ARUS about my idea and she was very encouraging! She told me that when I had finished it, to bring it to her and she would send it to the Deputy Warden of Programming. I needed also to make a list of the resources needed and supplies so that a cost could be put to the seminar, after all, money was always a consideration and how many days and what days and where it could be held. I was so excited!

I knew that I would need a copy of PsychopathFree by Peace, The Sociopath Next Door by Martha Stout, PH.D. and How To Survive The Loss of Love, A Guide to Overcome Your Emotional Hurts; Things to Do When There is Nothing to Be Done by Melba Colgrove PH.D., Harold H. Bloomfield MD., and Peter McWilliams. I went to the library and found two of the books and had my son send me a copy of PsychopathFree, which I considered to be the best book on the subject.

It took me three months to put it all together into a four session seminar. The time seemed to fly by and it kept me focused which help ease my anxiety. The hardest part wasn't the research, it was typing it up on the unit's typewriter which didn't have correction tape. I could only type so much in a day because my anxiety of not making mistakes kept my stomach in knots.

The day I had it sent off to the Deputy Warden of Programming was a day of triumph! I had worked hard and even through my bouts of anxiety and poor concentration, I did it! It was an accomplishment that I was proud of and I knew that I couldn't have done it without God guiding me. I was proud of the fact that even though I was in the middle of prison, my work ethic helped me to persevere. The only thing left was to wait to hear from the Deputy Warden.

I went back to writing this book and waited and waited. After three more months, it was obvious to me that I wasn't going to hear from her. I was so disappointed that she hadn't even acknowledged that she had received it! I believed God had given me the gift of putting the seminar together and I wasn't about to let it go to waste. I knew I would share it with my Facebook group when I was released, but the women in there, needed that information, now.

CHAPTER 11

I WANT TO LIVE!

I love you, LORD, my strength. The LORD is my rock, my fortress and my deliverer; my God is my rock, in whom I take refuge, my shield and the horn of my salvation, my stronghold. I called to the LORD, who is worthy of praise, and I have been saved from my enemies.
- Psalm 18:1-3

It was that time of the year. Red, White, and Blue and a "special" meal for the fourth of July. It was hot and muggy and standing in line was something I didn't relish, so to avoid the heat, I was still skipping quite a few meals and my bunkies always brought me fruit. It was also that time of year that I turned another year older, my birthday. I really didn't mind getting older, however, I didn't feel the need to announce it either. By this time, I had settled into a comfortable routine and didn't feel the need to change that. Other people, in particular, my bunkies had other ideas.

Right off the bat, before even getting out of bed, I was greeted to the happy birthday song. Each of the gals had made me a birthday card with well wishes. They were all creative and beautiful and heart felt. To top that off, my small circle of friends had paid to have a prison card made for me. Card making was a money maker for the artists behind the bars.

The card had my favorite color and my favorite animal, a dolphin. It was beautiful, a card that has never meant so much to me. In addition to the lovely card, they had made me a birthday cookie, made with peanut butter and fudge cookies. It was awesome. There is nothing like prison cooking and ingenuity.

It's strange to admit, but it was the best birthday I had ever had. Being surrounded by people who really cared and really wanted me to enjoy my special day. It's hard to say, but I had to go to prison to have my best birthday ever or at least in a very long time. The inmates that came together that day made me feel that I counted, that they were glad to know me. Outside that barbed wire, no had ever made my birthday special with the exception of my mother, who had died when I was thirty-six. I was a little bummed out that I hadn't received any birthday cards from the outside world. I just told myself that the mail in prison was a little behind.

It was a day to reflect. I was fifty-eight, alone and I had no purpose or direction to my life, I was adrift or so I thought at the time. I didn't know what to make of my life, what does one do with a difficult past? I was so grateful that God had always been with me, loved me, my only constant, yes, my rock. I was even more grateful that I had my J.O.B., giving me some sense of being needed and useful.

That night as I lay on my bunk, I pulled the covers over my head, it was the only way to feel like I had any privacy. In addition to that, our room was freezing because of being on a different thermostat. Everyone in the room, including me were wearing our coats, hats, and gloves over our pajamas. My brain was swirling, today had opened up a can of worms of emotions. I remember being sad and found that strange, given that I had such a wonderful day.

My internal dialog was asking a lot of questions. I had heard that there is a season for everything, I believed this was my season to learn and grow and the stretching wasn't going to be without pain. In my conversation with God that night, I asked if this was the time for me to grow. I certainly had the time to do it without a lot of worldly distractions. I knew that everything was in God's timing and His timing was always perfect.

Could it be that God had been trying to get my attention? Did God think I was ignoring Him and as a good Father, decided it was time to correct me? What better way to get my undivided attention than in prison, locked down most of the day. That was the first time that I entertained the idea that I was in prison so that God could direct my thoughts and actions? In all truth, I had been a disobedient daughter, actually a brat.

I started looking at my sentence as a blessing from God, a blessing of time to spend with Him. He loved me enough to send me there.

In the world, there are so many people, so many things that the Word of God has to compete with. I certainly wasn't dedicated enough to be diligent about communing with God, through prayer or anything else. As I pondered the last two years, I realized that I had never prayed to God to help me with this serious problem. Was it my ignorance that God loves to take care of the messes of our lives or was it my pride that I could take care of everything myself. I had lived so long, taking care of myself that it never occurred to me to ask God for help.

Something was happening inside of me, I could feel it, but I couldn't name it or identify what it was. I knew it felt positive, it felt right. It was the stirring of my soul, helping me to remember who I was, the daughter of the King. I didn't want to set my expectations too high and have them crash, like waves in the ocean on the rocks. I knew I was fragile and in recognizing that, I knew that I had to be careful. Life has no meaning without hope and I had lived without hope for so long. Did I dare to hope? I was mentally, physically and spiritually moving forward and I couldn't afford another setback, of any kind. I sensed for the first time that God had already worked out the future and that He was going to turn this mess into something good for me, after all, He is a very loving, kind and compassionate Father.

> **For I, the LORD your God, will hold your right hand, saying to you, 'Fear not, I will help you.'**
> **- Isaiah 41:13**

I was moving forward at a snail's pace in all areas of my life, mentally, physically and spiritually and couldn't afford a setback of any kind. I had seen it happen to other inmates, it looked like they were moving forward in a positive direction and then all of a sudden they took a different turn. Maybe that was how prison life was, always a huge sense of unbalance. All I could tell you is that I was staying faithful to God and the Word and had the sense that God had already worked everything out and that I didn't need to be anxious about it. This is a lot easier said than actually doing it.

It was about this time, a little after my birthday that when I went to receive my medications for the month at the medical center, something very strange happened. We were allowed to keep all maintenance medications in our lockers, it was only the psychiatric medications that had to be dispensed to us daily. As usual there was a long line and when I finally got up to the window, I noticed that the nurse wasn't our "regular" nurse, I had never seen her before. In addition to the monthly maintenance medications, she also handed me a 30 supply of Trazadone, my sleeping medication that I was given on a daily basis. I told her that I wasn't supposed to get them and she told me that yes, those were the orders. So, being an obedient prisoner, I put them with the rest of the medications and walked very slowly back to the unit. My mind was in a whirl, I knew I wasn't supposed to have them and yet I wasn't going to argue with the nurse. The outcome of doing that could have been worse than the medications being found in my locker.

It didn't take any time at all and I was consumed with thinking about those pills. To say I was obsessing would have been a mild statement. I knew that those pills were my one way ticket off the earth and out of prison. I sat on my bunk next to the locker and just stared and stared. I had never locked my locker unless I was going out of the unit, but now I kept it locked at all times. It is a wonder that none of my cellmates had noticed it, very little goes unnoticed in a cell with ten women.

I know that I had a couple of options, one was to sell them, and there was a good market for them. In fact, people "cheeked" taking their medication, not swallowing them, so that they could sell them. It was insane that people actually would buy a pill that had been in someone else's mouth. Selling them really wasn't an option for me, I didn't want to add drug dealer to my rap sheet. If I was caught I would go to segregation for I don't know how many days and I knew that I wouldn't do well in that situation and there was always the possibility of losing my parole.

I just sat there staring, sometimes with a blank mind and sometimes going over dying. It was a real struggle, I had wanted to die for so long and now I was given the opportunity. I knew that it wasn't God giving me that option, although, I knew He already knew how I was going to handle the situation. I had come to know that God allowed bad things to happen to good people, it wasn't a test as some might think, but a situation that allowed me to grow from the experience, so I would know how, I handled it. I had learned after praying for my second husband and being very exact as to what I wanted and needed and when Mr. Wrong showed up I thought God had answered my prayers...In my conversations with Him, He assured me that He wasn't the only one listening to my prayers! So, I was clear as to how this had occurred and believe me, I knew it was Satan, pure and simple.

You have to believe me, I was seriously considering this. I had all but given up hope for a future when God gave me that Bible and somehow, hope started to evade my thought processes. What did I really have to look forward to? Life as a felon wasn't going to easy and nothing was certain and I had made no plans other than I knew I wanted to move to Florida and get out of Michigan, my home state had not protected me and in my opinion the leadership was evil. I laughed at that, they aren't our leaders, they are our representatives, they work for us and yet it sure didn't feel that way.

I decided that I wasn't going to labor over the decision, I was going to come to an answer by the end of the evening. My thoughts seemed pretty clear cut. Looking back at it, I am amazed that someone contemplating suicide could do it so seemingly rational, no emotions involved, just hard facts.

I went through the day still obsessed with my locker and what was inside. The day seemed to drag, which was unusual because the days seemed to fly by. It was like I was out of my body, just going through the motions of what would look "normal."

I went to the medical center for my medications and it didn't surprise me that my Trazadone was given to me, confirming to me that it was a huge mistake to be given that sheet of pills. Again, I walked back to the unit slowly, knowing the time to make my decision was getting closer. It was a decision that either way, I was going to live or die with. I had never been a fence sitter and I wasn't going to start now.

When I got back to the cell, I laid down, facing the locker, focusing on those pills. I decided that I had better talk to God about this. I had "suicided" before, you notice I didn't say attempted…I wanted to die and was really mad at God when He didn't allow it. I knew I was fully capable of doing it.

I knew that God loved me, I have never had any doubt about it and I asked Him to forgive me, that I was so weak. I remember telling Him the pain just had to go and if dying meant that I would live in Hell for all of eternity, I was willing to chance that. I did admit that the pain had lessened and asked Him if I was just living with a "Fantasy of Dying." For as long as I could remember, I didn't want to be on this planet and had so many scenarios in my head. I laid there in silence, waiting for God to tell me what to do, praying, praying and praying…God didn't have to tell me what do, and I knew what I was going to do. I told Satan to be gone, that I wanted to LIVE!

LIVE, I wanted to LIVE…I had felt the glimmer of hope, a hope that I know could have only come from God. I didn't cry, I was very matter of fact with myself. I told myself to shut up with any thoughts or self-talk of suicide, I had my chance and I didn't take it, so there.

It was over, decision made and with it a peace that I had not known for quite some time, maybe never. In all honest, a little excitement was creeping into my thoughts. That night was a turning point in my life. With death no longer an option, I could put all of my energy into healing and living. Wow, what a difference twenty-four hours could make in a person's life. I didn't know what the future would hold for me, however, I knew that God did and I trusted Him enough to take it a day at a time and let my release on life unfold as He saw fit. For so long, I had taken charge of my life, maybe it was time to let God lead. I always laughed when someone said, LET GO, LET GOD…..were they nuts?

I had known since childhood that He had chosen me and now that I had given up the "suicide fantasy" I could get back on the path to my destiny that God wanted me on. I just had to trust and I did.

After that day, I started noticing the colors of the flowers that inmates had planted everywhere and heard the birds singing, of course, I think they were actually singing to me. Such a heavy weight had been lifted from me, everything was coming back into focus and I was so in love with my Father, all was good.

CHAPTER 12

GOD WANTED YOU TO HAVE IT

Do not be anxious about anything, but in every situation, by prayer and petition, with thanksgiving, present your requests to God. And the peace of God, which transcends all understanding, will guard your hearts and your minds in Christ Jesus.
- Philippians 4:6-7

It was a hot summer and I was so grateful for air conditioning, our cell was on a different air conditioner unit than the rest of Harrison. Not all units had it, in fact, most of our unit was hot because the air conditioner's condenser was broken. The rooms that were connected to that air conditioner were the rooms that housed the pregnant women. I was shocked, even though I shouldn't have been, that the prison didn't seem to care, even about pregnant inmates.

My prayer life was increasing and each day, I asked God to be with me and I felt His presence. I prayed for the women at WHV and the staff, my family and friends. I asked God to give me the strength to endure my time there and to keep me safe. I was reading my Bible and getting better acquainted with our Creator God.

Physically it seemed as though I was going backwards. I was so frustrated by the medical treatment or lack of, which I was receiving. I had been on thyroid medication since I was fourteen years old and the nurse practitioner who was in charge of my medical treatment decided that I didn't need it anymore and took me off of it.

I couldn't believe it then and still can't believe it now. During that time, my hair fell out in clumps, I was completely drained of energy, my bones and body ached, night sweats, and heart palpitations, just to name a few. During my monthly visit to my psychiatrist, he was not happy when I told him what was going on. I asked him, as a doctor if there was anything he could do and he sadly told me no. Even though thyroid was directly connected to my depression and mood, the facility didn't allow any holistic health care. He encouraged me to file a grievance about it.

At my monthly visit with the dietician, she told me the results from my last blood work, my cholesterol and triglycerides were significantly higher. When I told her about my thyroid situation, she was flabbergasted. She went over the blood work for thyroid and said she saw no reason for me to be taken off of the dosage of medication. She too encouraged me to grieve healthcare for not following proper protocol for the disease.

I filed the grievance and remember the day I was called to Healthcare to review it. The nurse told me that my blood work didn't support the need for medication at this time. I asked her if I had been miraculously cured of this disease. I knew with God, all things were possible. She just stared at me, not knowing what to say. She scheduled more blood work to collaborate her findings.

At the lab, I asked the nurse drawing my blood if he would want his mother receiving third world country medical attention, like I was. He told me, very cocky I might add, that no, his mother wouldn't do anything to get herself put in prison and did I really expect to receive top notch health care? I had to suppress my laughter and asked him what had happened to his oath to do no harm. It took two more months for me to be reinstated on the medication and at the same dosage. I found out later that my son had called the prison to register a complaint about my medical treatment.

On a hot August day, I was called out to the programs building, which was located on the west side. I had no idea what this was about. The itinerary didn't give any information. The heat was unbearable on the long walk over and the air conditioning in the building was so refreshing. I showed the guard my itinerary and he pointed to the row of seats at the end of the room. It wasn't long and a woman came towards me and asked if I was Ms. Faher. I told her yes and she asked me to follow her to the chapel's stock room. She then asked me if I was excited and I asked, what for? She smiled and told me the Bible that I had requested a year ago was finally here. I told her that was a mistake, I had only been there about five months. She looked puzzled and told me she would check the waiting list and be right back.

I stood there waiting for her to return. She came out of the stock room, grinning from ear to ear carrying the Bible. She told me that yes, I had clearly been on the list for a little over a year, and there was no mistake. I was stunned and speechless. As she handed me the Henry Morris Study Bible, the faux leather edition, she said "God wanted you to have this." I tried to smile through my tears as I checked out with the guard and walked back to my unit.

What had happened? I believed in miracles big and small, is that what happened here? I remembered that the inmate that had given me the used Bible when I was in RCG was also an aide to the Chaplain and I wondered if she had altered the waiting list for me to receive this gift. I definitely was going to ask her the first time I saw her again.

After returning to my unit and cell, I sat on the bunk and decided I wasn't going to waste this gift. I prayed a prayer of thanksgiving and sat there praising God, my Father. I turned to Genesis and started reading. It felt like it was the first time I had ever read the Bible, which it wasn't. I was seeing and understanding what I read with a much deeper insight. It was such an exciting time for me. What was even more amazing is that earlier in the day, I had told my bunkie that I was going to start a Bible study and it was obvious to me that God wanted me to have this study Bible to use as a reference. To say that God is AWESOME would be an understatement.

I was changing and I could feel it. I was less tense and anxious and to my amazement, I even smiled from time to time. I had asked and was now receiving my blessings. I had asked God to be with me, to let the words of my mouth be His truth, His light, His peace and His love.

I started that Bible study group and each day we could feel the presence of God with us. We used the Bible along with Our Daily Bread and two other daily inspirational books by Sarah Young, Jesus Calling and Jesus Today. Every day, without exception, something we were reading was exactly what someone in the group needed to hear. There was laughter, there were tears and by the grace of God, we found hope.

We met in the day room at one of the round tables in the back of the room. We didn't call it Bible study because no one was allowed to come together in numbers any larger than four. If we did, it might look like we were amassing to riot. I couldn't make this stuff up if I wanted to! Other inmates were watching T.V., playing games and talking. Everyone came to know that we would be there at 9:00 am. One of the strange phenomena that we experienced was, just at the exact moment we were reading and feeling the Holy Spirit, the noise level in the room skyrocketed, so we had to lean in, hold hands and talk louder. Sometimes we had to rebuke Satan in the name of Jesus Christ and slowly the room would calm down, the volume decreasing, allowing us to continue.

I am not exaggerating or overstating this, our Lord was so powerful, that He could change the environment in the room. This didn't just happen once, it was a frequent occurrence. With God on our side, who could be against us?

Each morning the group discussed how the rest of their day had gone and what blessings they had received. It was interesting that we received confirmation throughout the day, confirming God's word. When you live in prison and can feel and say you are blessed, that is a blessing indeed!

There were times when bad news would unsettle members of our group, which was ever flowing and ever changing, news like hearing that an appeal was not accepted or that anticipated money being put into their accounts didn't happen or the most common upsets came from telephone conversations. During those times we were able to be supportive to one another and remind each other that God was with us, even behind the barbed wire.

It was bound to happen and it did. One morning I went to the day room to prepare for the Morning Prayer group, I sat at our table and waited and waited and no one showed up. It was such an uneasy feeling. I could feel the other women in the room looking over at the "prayer" table wondering how long I would wait and what I would do. In addition to a core group that usually showed up, there were several women that never joined the table, but sat on the fringes, just listening, not participating but definitely paying attention. As the senior member of the unit, I felt it was important to be a positive role model for the other women and as they say, walk my talk. I got a cup of coffee, sat down and proceeded through the readings, prayer and praised.

After going through the material, prayers said, coffee gone, I went back to my cell and I could feel the anger creeping into my psyche. Didn't these women appreciate the time and effort I was putting in each day? I must have looked like a wet hen pacing back and forth in the cell. The few cellmates that were in the room, never said a thing. I just silently seethed, after all, these women obviously didn't know who they were dealing with! God must have had a good laugh and finally when He thought it was time to correct me, like any good father would, He asked me, "Did you think the Bible study was about you?" I stopped dead in my tracks and was stunned. God went on to explain that the study group was about Him and if anyone should be upset, it was Him and He wasn't upset. It was obvious that I was taking this personal and it wasn't about me. I couldn't possibly know what reasons people had for not attending, only God knew and if He was okay with it, I shouldn't lose a moment of peace over it. Why was I upset?

I took some time in the silence of the room to contemplate the whole situation and it was obvious to me that my ego had been bruised. I had a much higher opinion of myself and my pride was strutting about thinking I was more important than I really was. God is so amazing, He wasn't going to let me wallow in my self-absorption and after comforting me, told me I was going to do it again tomorrow and if again, no one showed up, I could continue with my own study.

There were organized Bible studies that were sanctioned by the prison, however, the waiting list was long and an opening only occurred when someone dropped out of a group. I was on that list and I was never called for the group during my stay.

It was not lost on me that trying to honor God was so difficult in prison and it seemed as though honoring Satan was so easy! The Television shows that were watched were full of naked people, there actually was a show with nudists dating each other, musical videos of people practically having sex with each other with music that probably made the devil blush. I don't consider myself a prude, but these shows were definitely over the top. There was no doubt what so ever, that prison was the Devil's playground.

The god of this age has blinded the minds of unbelievers, so that they cannot see the light of the gospel that displays the glory of Christ, who is the image of God.
- 2 Corinthians 4:4

For the wages of sin is death, but the gift of God is eternal life in Christ Jesus our LORD.
- Romans 6:23

CHAPTER 13

Justice Is Blind

I delight to do Your will, O my God, and Your law is within my heart." I have proclaimed the good news of righteousness in the great assembly; Indeed, I do not restrain my lips, O LORD, You Yourself know. I have not hidden Your righteousness within my heart; I have declared Your faithfulness and Your salvation; I have not concealed Your lovingkindness and Your truth from the great assembly. Do not withhold Your tender mercies from me, O LORD; let Your lovingkindness and Your truth continually preserve me. For innumerable evils have surrounded me; my iniquities have overtaken me, so that I am not able to look up; they are more than the hairs of my head; therefore my heart fails me. Be pleased, O LORD, to deliver me;

O LORD, make haste to help me! Let them be ashamed and brought to mutual confusion who seek to destroy my life; let them be driven backward and brought to dishonor who wish me evil.
- Psalm 40:8-14

Fall was finally settling on the prison. The mornings were crisp and you could see your breath with each step that you took. Even with all of the improvements to my health, walking any distance was still slow going, painful and exhausting. I was only going to the chow hall one time a day, usually at lunch time unless there was one of my favorite meals at dinner. Rarely did I go two times in one day.

One evening I was called the unit's base after I had taken my night medication. My legs were already starting to feel the effects, wobbly and not steady on my feet. My legs were always the first to relax before I fell asleep. The officer on duty told me I had been called to the control center which was the furthest place from the unit, to pick up legal mail. When I had first arrived, I had signed up to not give the prison permission to open it. At the time, I had no idea where I would be housed and at what time of day I would be called. Considering the shape I was in, I asked the officer if I could go in the morning and explained why I felt uncomfortable walking in the dark to the other side of the campus with legs that weren't at their best. She laughed at me and told me in no uncertain terms "Absolutely Not." I asked if someone could push me in the unit's wheelchair and again, "Absolutely Not."

I don't know how I made it there and back, but I did. Putting all of my effort into making it back to the unit, I hadn't even looked at the mail to see what it was or who had sent it. After getting back to the unit and plopping down on the bunk, tired and exhausted, I decided to find out what had taken me clear across campus at this hour and with me half drugged.

It was a letter from my appeals attorney and it was about the appeals committee board's decision to hear my appeal. Congratulations it said, the Court of Appeals found that my application for appeals had merit! Wow! It takes anywhere from eight to twelve months for the Court of Appeals to render its final decision.

I just sat there, re-reading it over and over. I had never felt so vindicated in my entire life. Both the appeals attorney and the Appeals Board felt that my case had merit. Finally, someone was going to be on my side and help me to get justice. I sat there feeling the warm tears of joy falling down on my still cold cheeks.

The next morning I decided to delve into the mountain of paperwork that had accompanied the letter. While I was no attorney, I gathered that the basis for the appeal was based on O.V. (Offender Violation) scores that had been incorrectly computed. The scores were used as guidelines for the sentencing. Whoa, I didn't know anything about O.V. scores, I remembered hearing the term bandied about, but had no clue what that meant and never asked. It appeared that as it was now, the range of incarceration was 7-23 months, with prison an option. Correctly scored the range would be 0-11 months of county jail time, which of course, with the jail having "Good Time," if I would have received the maximum, I would have been out in nine months!

I was so angry, I could have spit nails if they had been allowed in prison. The appeals paperwork leaned heavy on the fact that I had received ineffective counsel. Ineffective counsel! I paid my attorney up front $25,000 and he had not provided effective counsel! I was so angry, it now consumed me. All I could think of was getting even, but that was going to have to wait. My appeals attorney had advised me not to start any lawsuits until after I was re-sentenced. But for now, I was going to have to do up to another year before anything would be decided, how was I going to do that without going utterly insane?

Several inmates had told me that they didn't belong there either and after reading the appeals paperwork, there just might have been some truth to that. It was a real education on the legal system. I learned that money and attorney's egos along with those of the judges could make all of the difference in the outcome of a case. I also learned that if it was an election year, some cases were used as a poster child, I know that mine was. I was also told by other attorneys that justice was served differently if a Republican or a Democrat was serving it up. To think that politics should get in the way of justice, just sickens me. I remember asking my attorney if justice was always served and he told me certainly not. I believe that Lady Justice in the United States is blind, maybe she is even dead.

I started asking other inmates about their O.V. scores and no one knew what I was talking about. You would have thought that something that important would have be explained until the accused understood it. O.V. scores have such an impact on people lives! We aren't just an end to the means or are we?

> *Beloved, do not avenge yourselves, but rather give place to wrath; for it is written, "Vengeance is Mine, I will repay," says the Lord.*
> - **Romans 12:19**

My emotions were all over the place. I had joy that someone really understood the nightmare I had went through and was currently going through. I was so angry at my attorney, the judge, the prosecutor, and the Atty. General. None of them were looking out for my rights. I wanted revenge and was struggling with that. I kept taking it to God and sometimes that wasn't easy because I wanted results, NOW. God kept telling me to trust Him that He had already worked everything out and would take care of my enemies. He kept insisting that I focus on my recovery and on Him, after all, I had prayed that my heart's desire was to know Him more fully.

That summer, the prison was abuzz with news that the media had picked up on the fact that the prison was over-crowded. That was due in large part to the families of the inmates that were making their voices heard on behalf of their loved ones behind the barbed wire. It was so obvious at the Visitor Center, families had to wait for hours to be processed before they were re-united with their inmate. There were times that visits were cut short because there were no seats and there were still people waiting for their visit. There were actually times that visitors were turned away and the inmate sat waiting for hours until they were finally told that they had to go back to their unit, no visitors that day.

I had a problem in this area too. My step-father, who was 85 at the time waited for over two hours to see me and his insulin level dropped. He had thought he would have been processed and visiting me by this time. He had planned on eating lunch with me. He asked if he could go to his car where he had insulin in a mini-fridge and come back to his place in line. He was told that yes, he could leave and get his insulin, however, on returning, he would lose his place in line. He waited … When it was finally his turn to see me, he was stumbling, walking unsteady and a guard helped him to a seat. Of course I was angry but my first attention was to get him something to eat and drink. My step-father is a veteran and proudly wore his ball cap to show his allegiance to this country, he has never committed a crime and was treated so disrespectfully. When I complained to the C.O. in charge, she told me I could write a grievance, which I did and of course no action was taken because when I wrote the grievance, I didn't have the name of the officer in processing. I had the date and approximate time of the incident, but that wasn't enough.

As a tax payer, I too had no idea what was going on with the Michigan prison system, in fact, it would have never occurred to me to even look into it. I had never had a family member or friend involved with the system. Like most of the state's citizens, I was more aware of what was on McDonald's menu than anything to do with the state prisons. I had to give props to the families of felons that were trying to make a difference, they were relentless in bringing this to the attention of not only the media, but there were campaigns to state and federal agencies about the situation.

As inmates, we were kept in the dark about what activities were going on outside of the barbed wire. Inmate.com had reported that a local T.V. station in Detroit was doing an investigation into the matter and reporting it. We never got to see any of the reports, our cable connections mysteriously went haywire on the day and times of any airings. Once in a while there was a slip up and when we watched the news, there was a mention of something going on at the prison. On the days that the local papers ran articles about anything to do with the prison, those copies for those days didn't make it to the library. I was told that the reason for the security was the prison officials didn't want a riot.

Of course, like most things in life, there is always a way around anything and this was no different. Inmates from Lansing, Grand Rapids and other areas were having their local newspapers delivered to them. If it wasn't front page news, it got by the eyes checking on our mail. By the time I got to read some of the papers, they were crumpled and dirty having made it all around the campus. It appeared that there were reporters out there that cared and wanted the public to know what was going on. The problem was how to get the public to care if they didn't have a loved one incarcerated. The prevailing attitude was and is, "I am safe because 'they' are locked up."

One morning I awoke to hear our unit officer yelling, which wasn't unusual, however, this was louder than most mornings. We were to have our cells cleaned up and in regulation order. We all had a list on the back of the cell doors what was expected and on most days, there were some areas that were relaxed, however, this day wasn't one of them. When I walked into the hallway there was a flurry of activity, unit porters were washing the walls and ceilings. No place was going to be overlooked. This could have meant only one thing, a horse and pony show. Our unit, Harrison was the smallest unit, so it was easier to get into tip top shape and was the unit that the warden used for show and tell. He would lead them in and direct them out usually as quickly as he could. Rarely did the visitors make any eye contact with us, it was as if we weren't there. And never were they led to areas that might show MDOC in a bad light, for example the mold in the showers or water fountains that didn't work.

As everyone was doing their chores, they were whispering that the group coming through would be headed by a former warden there, which had been promoted to a position over all of the facilities and worked in Lansing, the state's capital.

I don't know how inmates know what is going on, but there were a lot of times that they were right and this was one of them. Everyone on the east side remembered the former Warden and said she was pro-inmate as opposed to the current warden who was anti-inmate. To say they were excited about the visit would have been an understatement. They all said that if anyone could make a difference and shed light on the overcrowding situation, it would be her. A lot of what ifs were exchanged and the whole east side was abuzz with anticipation.

I learned later that the inmates on the west side, the long termers, had been skeptical. They said they had seen and heard all of this before and laughed at the east for even thinking for a minute that anything would change.

As it turned out, the day of the big visitation, I was sitting in the day room watching the television when the group came in. It was indeed, the former warden and her entourage, including the current warden. Each member of the group must have been instructed to make no eye contact and ignore our presence because that is exactly what they did. The group didn't go any further than the officer's base. They all stood in a semi-circle facing the C.O., listening as the ex-warden talked. Behind the base was the ten cell room I was housed in that had been converted from the unit's T.V. room to the cell and next to that the unit's counselor's office which had been turned into a six bed cell. Not one of them looked in or asked any questions. Directly behind them was the bath and shower rooms. There were only three out of the four toilets working. The showers were not only full of black mold, but the ceiling had peeling paint hanging down. They reminded me of the pictures that had been taken at the Veteran's Administration Hospitals.

The cells might have been clean but beneath the military made bunks were mattresses that were old, flat and cracked with who knew what was inside of them. They never adventured into the T.V. and quiet room combo to see what happens to appliances that are over used. The ice machine was broken and out of the two microwaves, one was broken.

What made all of it deplorable was the fact that the unit had originally been built for fifty-two inmates and now housed sixty-eight, with the same number of toilets and showers. To make matters worse, the unit's handicapped bathroom & shower was being used as a storage room. The end result was that there were long lines for the toilets, showers, microwaves, hot pots etc. There was a grooming room which only could have four inmates at a time and again, at peak times, there was a line for that.

This was just my unit and the entire prison was as crowded, in fact, some of the housing units were even more over-crowded. Over-crowding was real, getting worse daily and wasn't going away soon. The result of long medication lines is that sometimes they had to be cut short for count and were resumed late at night, throwing all of us off of our schedules. I remember one night being expected to go to the medication line at midnight, which I didn't go to. The chow lines were backed up which took a toll on all inmates with a lot of cutting in line which aggravated everyone, especially with C.O.'s watching and not caring.

The toll on the staff was obvious, there was an inmate to officer ratio that had to be maintained and MDOC had a shortage of staff which meant that C.O.'s were mandated to work extra shifts back to back. It was not uncommon for me to find the officer on duty at night, sound asleep when I went to the bathroom.

The talk at the chow hall, on the walkways and on the big and small yards was all about the same thing, the visit. As I saw the entourage leave, I thought what a shame, if the other units had the same horse and pony show, what a missed opportunity for the people in "charge" of us to make a difference for many inmates. There had been so much optimism for the visit, however, I didn't have a good feeling about it, with all that I had seen.

The next day, in phone conversations with family and friends on the outside, many were reporting the same thing. The former warden had been interviewed in Lansing, stating that

Women's Huron Valley Correctional Facility wasn't over-crowded! It was devastating news to the entire east side population. The west side didn't have much to say, they didn't believe that anything would be done. The atmosphere was like the air had been let out of all of us, we were deflated, almost hopeless, no one was listening or caring.

That fall, I saw more changes that weren't positive for the inmates. Many inmates had been able for years to purchase regular clothes for wearing on visits. It was especially great when the visitors were the children of the inmates. That right was taken away and all of us had to wear the state issued blues. The only time that the regular clothes could be worn was the day the inmate was released. Some women had spent a lot of money on these clothes over the years and now they were banned. This was especially hard on the west siders since they had purchased the most clothing over the years. In addition to visits, state blues had to be worn to medical lines and the chow hall.

About a month later, news was spread about the former warden giving another interview and she actually back pedaled a bit on her stance about WHV not being over-crowded. Those inmates that got the Lansing News were able to see the interview in print. She stated that WHV could handle more inmates because the old chow hall was being refurbished to house 120 inmates. It was so ridiculous, it wasn't even funny. Even if that building gave the prison an extra 120 beds, it wouldn't make a difference at medical lines or at the chow hall. It wouldn't make a difference for programs that had long waiting lists also.

My bunkie was on the work crew that was doing the refurbishing, again another project with prisoner labor. She said the design was like the federal prisons, with only partial walls and no doors. Before being refurbished as a kitchen, the building had been a gymnasium, resulting in a lot of echoing which wasn't noise "friendly." It didn't surprise me when there was an electrical fire and the sewers were continuing to back up. The new unit was called Leelanau, it didn't have a small yard and the social room was very small.

It was about this time that my morning call out sheet contained an appointment with the Boot Camp Staff (SAI). I was stunned, again, another announcement coming out of the blue.

After being housed on the SAI floor when I first arrived in prison, I swore that I would NEVER go through boot camp! The mere thought of standing before those C.O.'s sent shivers up and down my spine. I recognized that not only was I new to prison then, but that I had been further traumatized by not only their behavior but by what I observed them doing to trainees.

Because it was on my call-out sheet, I had to go, whether I wanted to or not. As I walked toward Unit 9, I could feel the anxiety increasing, even making breathing a little difficult.

Once inside the gate and checked in at the desk, I was told the meeting would be the day room. I took one of the last chairs, which of course had to be up front and center, directly in from of the podium. Oh boy, it appeared that nothing was going to be easy.

It was the same Lieutenant that stood erect and very direct when I was first admitted that was giving the welcome to boot camp speech. As I before had mentioned, I admired her tall, straight back posture, however, her voice was reverberating down to my soul.

She told us that each of us had been selected for the opportunity to participate in the six week program and that if we graduated, we would be released, with a tether. In other words, get out of prison early!!!

I sat there as she explained the program and knew that I would say yes. I even laughed at myself for being such a hypocrite. I had been very vocal that there was nothing that could induce me to sign on to this program. Nada, no way! I guess I had been there long enough to recognize a way to get out of this evil.

After signing the paperwork we were told that our sentencing judge would be notified that the prison had offered us this program and we had accepted the opportunity. She kept saying it was an opportunity, that not everyone was offered a slot on the roster.

As I checked out and returned to my unit, I thought I must have been crazy. Did I really think that I could withstand that kind of in-your-face yelling? Did I really think I could withstand the demeaning way the trainees were treated? Did I really think that I could pass the rigorous physical training? The Lieutenant had mentioned that the staff were aware of limitations for some of the trainees and that it would be taken into consideration. If we were kicked out of the program for legitimate medical reasons, it would not be held against us.

At the same time that I was anxious about the prospect of going through the program, I was excited that I had been chosen and could actually leave early, even if it was with an ankle monitor.

All of my cell mates wanted to know how it went and if I had said yes. So I explained what I had learned and finally told them that yes, I had signed the paperwork, that it was a done deal unless my judge denied me the opportunity. As I said those words, I had a sudden dread, what if she did say no, and what then?

Of course everyone had an opinion about it and the one thing that everyone pretty much agreed on was that due to the overcrowding, the prison was pushing more and more people to go through the program which opened up bed space. They said the biggest clue was that they were willing to accept people with limited mobility and make allowances for it. Another clue was that they had increased their program's size to accommodate more trainees.

I wrote a letter to my appeal's attorney about the offer and within a week, he showed up to tell me in person, to take the offer, because it was still another year before my appeal would even be heard. That still astounded me, if they knew I didn't belong here, what was the reason that I had to stay so long?

In the end, it was all a mute-point, my judge denied my application and left no remarks as to why and if it would be accepted at a later date.

In talking with God about all of this, He assured me that it would all work out, according to His plan. His plan! Had He planned this prison time? I really was coming to accept that, begrudgingly anyway.

CHAPTER 14

The Big Move

*I called on the L*ORD *in distress; The L*ORD *answered me and set me in a broad place. The L*ORD *is on my side; I will not fear. What can man do to me? The L*ORD *is for me among those who help me; therefore I shall see my desire on those who hate me. It is better to trust in the L*ORD *than to put confidence in man. It is better to trust in the L*ORD *than to put confidence in princes.*
- Psalm 118:5-9

Before I knew it, the Christmas season was fast approaching. I could usually ignore it, however, every commercial on the T.V. had Christmas all over it. The ringing candy Kisses were starting to get to me. Reminding me that I would be away from my family and friends. The unit representatives had decorated the social room. A tree was in the corner, no lights were allowed, but it was festive. You could definitely feel the changed atmosphere, everyone was making presents and I actually got into making Christmas cards, for people in here and on the outside. I have always been crafty and was able to use that skill.

I had a small circle of friends, although I don't know if that is the proper term for them. They were not going home with me and I wasn't going to stay in contact with them once I was released. It is so strange how some inmates labeled people in their circle as, "That's my baby daddy, that's my mother, that's my girl, that's my wife, my boo, etc." I found that it was a way to create a family and in some cases, these circles were their families. It was a reason that many inmates came back to prison, that is where their family was.

It was interesting how these allegiances quickly changed, one day a friend or family member and the next day an enemy. The line between the two was actually very small. I had come to expect the unexpected.

The unit, Harrison, which I was housed in was intended for pregnant inmates, which meant there was a lot of drama on a daily basis and circles changed quickly, sometimes hourly. Up to that point, I had no difficulty in keeping my opinions to myself, but that was starting to become more difficult. I know that my years of infertility were probably behind most of the opinions that I had about the women that were pregnant and in prison. I viewed my son as a gift from God, He had entrusted me with this treasure and it would be for a short time. I did everything I could to help him become a healthy, happy, well-adjusted human being, a productive member of society, a giver, not a taker.

I was so saddened at what I saw there and by what I heard. Many of the women in there had other children and in a lot of cases, they didn't even know where they were. Many of the children had different baby daddies and even more shocking was the fact that many of those children had also been born in prison. I actually had an inmate tell me that she got better pre-natal care and that she wasn't using drugs while in prison, helping the child growing inside of her. I remember asking her how she timed it to come back to prison and she told me she violated her probation, once she knew she was pregnant.

It also saddened me how self-centered many of the women were. Most of them talked about what they would do when they were released. The talk was about getting weaves, getting their nails done, getting the newest iPhone, and eating at the most expensive restaurant that they could find. The next topics of discussion were the luxury vehicles, clothes, shoes, purses, everything of course a named brand. What struck me as very odd was that very few talked about being reunited with their baby and their other children. They weren't worried about how they were going to support their children or how being separated would have affected them. I actually asked how they were going to support their children and was told that WIC, food stamps, Medicaid, etc. would take care of it all.

I should have bit my tongue, but as I wrote earlier, my tolerance was shorter and shorter for stupid people. I actually said, "So, along with other tax payers, you are supporting your children." Even stranger is the fact that they didn't have a clue as to what I was inferring. I wanted to yell that I, as a tax payer was actually supporting their children, but I was sane enough to know that would not be a good idea.

I wanted my son to do better in life than I had. I wanted so much for him. It was obvious that these women didn't want anything different for their children. Our priorities could not have been further apart. Their priorities were expensive sneakers, clothes and cars, not what they could be doing to enhance the lives of their children. Somehow, someway, there will have to be an honest dialogue on these issues or segments of the population will continue, disenfranchised and returning to the revolving door of prison.

The weather was colder and it had snowed a couple of times giving the appearance of a winter wonderland with Christmas soon approaching. With all of the beauty around us, we were cold, wind-blown, not having the proper attire for the weather. Everywhere that we went was by foot and most of us were wearing the same shoes we had in summer, the same coat we had in summer as our rain coat. I became acquainted with long johns and they almost became my second skin. Many of us slept with our coats, caps and gloves on to keep warm. The buildings were heated with steam heat and the temperature was set low. I prayed to God that once I got out, I never wanted to be cold again.

It was the twenty-second of December when I was called to the base after the evening meal. It was dark out with the son setting around 5 0'clock. I felt anxious, every time that I had been called to the base at this time of day, it was only bad news and this time it wasn't any different. I wasn't prepared for what came next, I was told to pack my duffel bag, that I was being moved to another unit. I was dumb founded! I had never been in trouble, the staff pretty much ignored me, which was a good thing. There were three of us that moved that night.

We piled our belongings onto a cart and then we were told we were moving to Dickenson, the biggest unit on the grounds. My anxiety went through the roof, I felt sick. We took turns pulling the heavy laden cart. There was fresh snow on the sidewalk and in some areas ice had formed. We were all in shock, it was like we were walking ghosts, very little was said. I kept asking myself, how this could be happening,

There were four blocks within Dickenson, A, B, C and D. The building was a two story and of course, I had been assigned to C block which was upstairs. I never dreamed that I would be moved and had never got a no stair detail. Thankfully, we were allowed to use the elevator to haul our duffel bags to our newly assigned cells. I kept asking God for a good bunkie, He had answered my prayers before and I hoped that it wouldn't be any different.

My new bunkie was a Christian and I felt so blessed to be assigned to that cell. I was close to the bathrooms and close to the stairs. She was on top and I was on the lower bunk. The room was spacious and the lockers were larger than I had had before. I was almost done un-packing when a C.O. came to the cell and told me to pack up, that I was being moved to another cell. What? It was late, I was chilled to the bone and I was near collapsing, the walk over and up those stairs had nearly wiped out all of my energy. Both I and the new bunkie were so disappointed. Evidently, they had someone different for that cell.

In slow motion, I packed up and was led down another hallway to the new cell. It was a four bed cell and to make matters worse, I was assigned the top bunk! I kept saying, "This can't be happening." I went through my paperwork and showed the officer my bottom bunk detail from Medical. She looked it over and told me that it had expired at the end of September and asked why I hadn't had it renewed. EXPIRED? I was stunned and told her I didn't know the detail had an expiration date other than when I was released.

I was told that I would have to stay on the upper bunk until I could have a new one issued. I could feel any energy that I had left, completely leave me. I remember all too well how difficult it had been to get the first detail issued. With each step I took towards my new cell my mind was shutting down along with my body. In all actuality, if I had known what waited for me in that cell I would have fainted dead away. It only would be through God's grace that I would be able to continue on my path to freedom.

When I arrived back at the cell, I sat down in my designated desk chair. I just sat there, stiff and barely able to move, wondering how I was going to make it up while the other three cellmates talked as if I wasn't even there. If I had been expecting any kind of greeting, I would have been very mistaken. My senses were alert to something I couldn't put a name on.

I threw the sheets and blanket on top of the bunk and started the slow ascent up the ladder. As I was climbing I was reminded how difficult it had been when I first arrived to climb the ladder. It was a little easier now due to the weight I had lost, however, I still had no strength or balance. My bunkie below me started talking to me, that I had better get moved to another cell with a lower bunk available, she didn't want to see me fall. It wasn't concern for me that I heard, it was more like a command. Once I was up there, I just collapsed. I didn't make the bed or put on my pajamas. It was a night full of my restless legs twitching and with me tossing and turning. As tired as I was, I couldn't shut my brain off and all of the little energy I had left was used to hold back the sobs that were deep in my throat.

Looking for the positive, the room was much warmer than my cell at Harrison, I wouldn't have to sleep with my coat and hat on, that was a good thing since they were both laying over my desk chair and I wasn't about to get down. I also learned that the handicap bathroom was next to our cell and we could use it. That was a blessing!

The next morning when I awoke, I heard my bunkie below me moving around, so I hung my head over and said, "Good Morning!" Immediately she snapped back that she hadn't given me permission to talk to her and not to talk to her and told me directly that I hadn't even brushed my teeth, so what gave me the impression it was alright for talking. Okay, this was definitely something that I didn't expect. The other two bunkies had gone to breakfast, so it was just the two of us.

After going down the ladder to the bathroom, which was harder than going up, I returned to the cell to make the bed and start my daily devotions. My new bunkie just glared at me with hatred. It was obvious to me that she didn't like me and considered me weak so that she could bully me. I knew who and what she was, a bully, someone who had lived their life in darkness and hated the light that was shining from me. In all my time at WHV I had never and would never have such evil directed at me. She continued to badger me when no one else was in the room, exactly how bullies operate. I had asked God to surround me with His angels and I trusted that they were there.

It was getting harder for her since her demeanor wasn't working on me as she would have liked. The next morning, in a loud voice, she asked me if I ever left the cell. I told her I didn't have a lot of call outs and pretty much stayed in the cell. She told me in no uncertain terms that I needed to get out and give her space. She couldn't function without having alone time. It was laughable since the other bunkie, who as it turned out, was new to the cell having arrived only hours before me, never left. She didn't even go the T.V. room, she just laid on her bunk and watched her T.V., read or slept. I just laughed which made her all the madder. She tried to throw me under the bus one morning when I was getting hot water for my coffee and the C.O. was inspecting the cells. I had left a blanket unfolded on the made bed knowing I would be returning to it to continue with my devotionals. When I got back to the cell, she told me I was getting a ticket and that I needed to go the base to receive it. What! I went to the base and the C.O. told me I had not emptied the trash next to my desk and that the blanket was out of order. I had never received a ticket and wasn't going to now. I asked her to come back to the cell, that the trash can in question wasn't my trash can, it was used by everyone in the room. The minute we got to the cell, the bully started talking trash about me. I turned, looked at the C.O. and told her that I was being bullied and that I wouldn't stand for it. Of course she was doing what bullies do, asked the other cellmate if she was bullying me and of course there was a quiet no and she said that she didn't think so. I could tell she just wanted to cover her butt and not make Jessica mad so she would go after her.

I didn't get a ticket and never got a ticket for my entire time at WHV, the C.O. was smart enough to see what was happening. I learned later that the inmate who had the bunk I was assigned to, had been moved to another cell because she was being bullied. That is the way the system worked, move the victim and leave the bully alone. It is laughable even today.

When it was time, my bunkie was moved to the "going home" unit until it was her time to be released. It was at that time that I was moved to her bunk. Everything seemed to be working out, after all.

I was spending more and more time in the Word, ignoring everything that was going on around me and there was plenty. As it turned out, the other three cellmates were gay. I didn't know if they were at home, but they definitely were in there. It was no wonder that they felt the need to attack me, I was a Christian and not afraid to speak the Word or its truth.

Luckily, I had found a few other Christian women and we met daily in the day room for Bible study and to play cards. It was the only way I could keep my sanity.

CHAPTER 15

The Life Of A P.O.A.

*Hear my prayer, O L*ORD*, and let my cry come to You. Do not hide Your face from me in the day of my trouble; Incline Your ear to me; In the day that I call, answer me speedily. For my day are consumed like smoke, And my bones are burned like a hearth. My heart is stricken and withered like grass, So that I forget to eat my bread. Because of the sound of my groaning my bones cling to my skin.*

I am like a pelican of the wilderness; I am like an owl of the desert. I lie awake, And am like a sparrow alone on the housetop.

My enemies reproach me all day long; those who deride me swear an oath against me. For I have eaten ashes like bread, And mingled my drink with weeping, because of Your indignation and Your wrath; for You have lifted me up and cast me away. My days are like a shadow that lengthens, And I wither away like grass.

But You, O LORD, shall endure forever, And the remembrance of Your name to all generations. You will arise and have mercy on Zion; for the time to favor her, yes, the set time, has come. For Your servants take pleasure in her stones, And show favor to her dust. So the nations shall fear the name of the LORD, And all the kings of the earth Your glory. For the LORD shall build up Zion; He shall appear in His glory. He shall regard the prayer of the destitute, And shall not despise their prayer.

This will be written for the generation to come, that a people yet to be created may praise the LORD. For He looked down from the height of His sanctuary; from heaven the LORD viewed the earth, to hear the groaning of the prisoner, to release those appointed to death, to declare the name of the LORD in Zion, And His praise in Jerusalem, when the peoples are gathered together, And the kingdoms, to serve the LORD. He weakened my strength in the way; He shortened my days.

I said, "O my God, do not take me away in the midst of my days; Your years are throughout all generations. Of old You laid the foundation of the earth, And the heavens are the work of Your hands. They will perish, but You will endure; yes, they will all grow old like a garment; like a cloak You will change them, And they will be changed.

But You are the same, And Your years will have no end. The children of Your servants will continue, And their descendants will be established before You."
- Psalm 102:3

One of the things I liked about my new cell were the huge windows that faced south. They let in the light which warmed the heart and toes on a cold winter's day. I could sit on the bunk and watch as the inmates went to and fro, the main street was directly in front of the unit. At night, the moon and stars could put on quite a show. It seemed to me that all of creation was smiling, just for me. I was finally feeling a sense of the routine, which was important for all inmates, it was the only stability that we could count on.

My bunkie continued to bully me and I continued to ignore her, at least as much as I could. She ran a "store" out of our cell which meant people were always at the door and in some cases, the buyers just walked in. I didn't like it and it was forbidden, however, the C.O.'s had to know that she was running it and were looking the other way. It was a two for one, I hadn't been aware of any in Harrison, however, I was told that most units had at least one. We had two, a unit representative was running one also.

One night, one of the usual buyers came in and laid down with her and I had to listen to the cooing and kissing. I guess she was more than a buyer and I wondered how much more of that I was going to have to put up with. I didn't have to wait long to find out. That inmate and one of my other bunkies were caught on the west side, which was a major ticket for being out of place and resulted in both of them having to go to segregation for at least a month. Poor bunkie, the only person that she seemed to genuinely like or at best tolerated, was that bunkie, they had been the longest in cell together.

With a bunk opened up, it didn't take long before a new inmate was assigned to the cell. The dynamics of the room changed drastically, however, I was happy with the new bunkie, we were about the same age, she was straight and a Christian. The new bunkie worked in the kitchen and was rarely in the cell. She didn't have a television, so I let her watch mine when I wasn't in the room. A few nights a week, we both liked the same programs and shared the earphones to listen together to the programs.

Back when I was in my first assigned unit, Harrison, I found out about a position that wasn't classified as a job, but a program. It was called Prisoner Observation Aide or POA for short. It was a position that you had to be recommended to by someone on the staff. After looking at the requirements and the duties of a POA, I was determined that I was going to become one.

The position would require me to sit for three plus hours, depending on the need, to observe prisoners that were locked down, segregated and were either a danger to themselves or to others. Every fifteen minutes it was documented as to what the prisoner was doing. Depending in the shift that was worked, the activity to be reported could be just about none, for example, the night shift when they were sleeping or day shift at meals and medications time. The position required complete confidentiality, dedication and compassion for those that were being held, sometimes against their will.

I wrote a page as to why and what I could bring to the position and turned it into the C.O. in the unit that would be doing the recommending. I knew that, as with everything else, it would take time and time was something that I had plenty of. It took about three months before I heard that I had been accepted into the program. I remember being excited, it would bring purpose back to my life, it would make the days go by faster, and it would look good to the parole board and the fact that it was the highest paying prisoner position, didn't hurt at all. The position paid $3.12 a day, no matter how many hours were worked. I couldn't wait to start.

After a day of training and shadowing with another POA, and she had been at WHV for seventeen years, I was on my own. There was nothing that could have prepared me to the pain, suffering and horror of what I would observe and yes at times, the sheer stupidity that some prisoners used to purposely be put there. As I sit here writing this, my brain seems to be jumbled. I can only attribute it to the trauma that I witnessed and the ensuing trauma related to my own PTSD.

My shift was 9:30 a.m. to 12:30 p.m. and I usually worked about four times a week. It always varied depending on how many prisoners were sequestered away and how many POA's were available. The closer to holidays always seemed to increase the population, which meant that I sometimes worked seven days a week.

To describe the typical prisoner just couldn't be done, there was nothing typical about any of it, from the prisoners to the staff. It was a little world unto its own. The staff usually fell into two different camps, those that appreciated what we did, therefore lessening their duties and actually being respectful of the POA's and the other camp that felt that POA's were taking away what officers should be doing and didn't like the idea that a POA would think they were special in anyway, always reminding us that we too, were prisoners. It took me a while to figure out which camp everyone belonged to, but it sure made my life easier once I figured it out. I had to remind myself daily that whatever and wherever I was placed, I would get through it and be able to go back to my cell to crash.

There were several units that housed these prisoners and with the exception of one, was on the east side. The one on the west side was in the prison's segregation unit, it was a place that I dreaded and fortunately, I wasn't assigned to it on a regular basis.

The west side of the prison is the oldest side of the campus and is where in addition to segregation, the lifers are housed. I could always feel the change in energy when I stepped through the gates to this side. I could never put a name to it, I just felt it.

All of the cells in this unit had the toilet/sink inside, there were no communal restrooms, as there were on the east side. The paint was peeling everywhere, in fact, I peeled some paint chips from a door I was sitting in front of, while I was watching a prisoner. Someone had asked me if I could get some samples, there was a group that was covertly collecting evidence of what was wrong in the prison. This was a part of the lead paint project. There was no air-conditioning in this unit and in the winter, it felt like there was no heat. The first time I saw the cement beds with the metal loops for restraints, I thought it looked like they belonged in a horror movie.

The plastic mattresses were well worn and the padding inside was compressed and thin. I couldn't imagine trying to get any sleep on it. There were no sheets or pillows for that matter. Some of the windows were cracked and if there was a screen on the window, there were a lot of holes in it. It didn't help that the prisoners wore a one piece "gown" with Velcro, no underwear or socks.

In addition to the graffiti everywhere, there were holes on all of the walls. There were actually a couple of cells that the holes were bored completely through the block walls and the prisoners were able to talk to the prisoner in the next cell.

The first inmate that I want to shed some light on had been in the isolation cell for over two years. From the first time to last time that I observed her, I felt so much compassion, I know that God wanted me just to show this prisoner love, peace and truth.

The first day I observed her she was talkative, very inquisitive, which I understood because the POA's were her life line to what was happening on the outside. It was obvious that she knew the routines and the staff members and when they didn't respond to her requests/demands she became very insistent. There was such an innocent sweetness about her, which I felt was genuine.

My understanding was that about two years ago, she found out that her twin sister had died and she just lost it. She was put into isolation because she kept banging her forehead into the cement wall. I could still see where the scar, about four inches long and running along the part in her beautiful auburn hair. I asked why it looked so fresh and was told that she had recently went through a rough patch and started banging her head.

As the weeks and months went by, it was so obvious that this woman needed to be in a mental institution, not prison. Yes, she had committed a crime, arson, however, it had to be obvious at the time of sentencing that she needed help and prison wasn't the place she would receive it.

Each of the prisoners were assigned a therapist, who visited them about twice a week and made sure that they were receiving the proper medications. When a therapist came to visit, I had to move my chair next to the door, while the "session" was going on. Since my back ground had been in social work, I was stunned to hear what was or wasn't going on. It was that way for each prisoner that I observed and was there when a therapist came for their "session." I finally got the nerve to ask a therapist about it and was told that they weren't there to help the inmates to stabilize or help them with their mental illnesses, they were there to make sure that they would be more manageable. I remember having to put on a mask of calmness because, underneath, I was raging mad.

This inmate's therapist let her have a book in the cell and had given her a few crayons with one of those black and white composition books. She was writing a novel, mostly in her head and was encouraged to write it down. I told her I had written and published a book, so she liked to share with me where she was at in the story line. It didn't take too long to realize the beautiful princess was her twin sister and this was her way in not only dealing with her death, but a way to staying in touch with her. There was a handsome prince, I was never able to pinpoint who he really was, but I was sure that he was based on a real person.

She shared some of her life story with me. I ascertained that she had always been mentally ill and it was ignored as she bounced from one foster family to the next. She had never had anyone in her corner fighting for her or for that matter even caring. She had a grandmother that was all I knew about her family. Since her incarceration, she had never received a letter, phone call or visit.

As it was now, she received her meals in a styrofoam box and only food that could be eaten with her fingers were served to her. The POA's were a great source of encouraging her, being positive in this place of darkness. If she could show that she wasn't a danger to herself she could have full meals with plastic sporks and served on a regular tray.

Just when I thought it looked like she was on a path to stabilizing, I walked in to find her in full restraint gear, straps attached to those iron rings on the side of the bed. I could see her fighting with all her strength to get up. It was obvious that she had split her head open once again, the blood was matted in her hair and forehead.

It didn't take long for the nurse to come in with syringes of medication to, as I saw it, shut her down and that is what happened within a few minutes. It is something to see, because the nurse can't be in the room alone with her, there were two C.O.'s escorting her. I remember sitting there and just praying for this woman. I asked God to be with her in this, yet another hour of need.

This was a cycle that she would repeat over and over again. It would look like she was stabilizing and bam, she was banging her head on the wall. It would start with her talking to people that only she could see and hear. I asked if she would be released on her release date even if she wasn't stabilized and told no, she had to be stabilized in order to be released, since Michigan had closed all of the mental institutions. It looked like she was going to live her lifetime in that cell. There was no one to be an advocate for her.

There was another inmate that was very quiet, very paranoid and fearful of everyone with the exception of one C.O. that treated her like a human being. She was in isolation because she kept trying to escape. If she ever needed to come out of her cell, a Captain had to escort her.

She rarely ate, she believed that she was being poisoned. She had lost quite a bit of weight, her spine was starting to show. Some of the CO's let her keep her tray and like a mouse in the night, she would come out to nibble on the now, cold food. There were others however, that took her tray away if she didn't eat it at the "appropriate" time.

She wasn't very talkative and she spent her days trying to figure a way to get out. One day when I was observing another prisoner a couple of cells down, she used her blanket to turn on the sprinkler in her cell, this was actually the second time she had done it. She had barricaded the door so it would be difficult to get into the cell to turn it off. That day she flooded each cell and the hallway had about three inches of dirty water in it.

It was the POA's that had to push the water out of the hall through the door at the end of the hall. It was hard work and the water just kept coming. All of the inmates had to sit on their cots to stay dry. Of course this situation was just an excuse for them to act out. It was like a zoo. Finally a maintenance man came and shut the water off at the water main until they could get into the room to repair the sprinkler head. I was so glad when that day was over.

One of the most difficult women to observe was in her sixties, a former prostitute from Grand Rapids MI where she was arrested. She had the diagnosis of schizophrenia and her mood swings were wide and often. On her good days she recited scripture and sung old time gospel songs. On her less than good days she yelled, "Get me out" over and over. She was always hungry and wanted more to eat. There were a few C.O.'s that would give her the left over trays if someone didn't want one. In her calm moments, she was a sweet woman. She and I got along fabulously. We actually had been cell mates in the ten bed cell. When she wouldn't get up to go to the bathroom and urinated in her bed, we complained, she finally was moved to another unit. It was sad how the system just passed her along.

She finally got moved to the 'mental' unit and was actually doing very well there until she got a bladder infection and started spitting of the C.O.'s. She was then moved into a segregated unit for a closer watch. I can still remember her beautiful voice, like a song bird singing to God. I laugh now, remembering when a man came onto the floor, she perked right up, she loved men. They tried to ignore her but that was next to impossible.

My position as a P.O.A. gave me a few perks, I got to cut into the chow line if I was called to work and wouldn't have time to eat, if I didn't. Most of the C.O.'s were fine with that, however, there were those C.O.'s that let you know that on their watch, they weren't going to let us cut. Most of the C.O.'s were okay with the P.O.A.'s and there were some that wanted to remind us we were prisoners and don't start thinking we were anything else.

CHAPTER 16

OH HEAR ME

O Lord my God, if I have done this: if there is iniquity in my hands, if I have repaid evil to him who was at peace with me, or have plundered my enemy without cause, let the enemy pursue me and overtake me; yes, let him trample my life to the earth, and lay my honor in the dust.
- Psalm 7:1-5

My life was anchored by studying the Word of God early every morning. In fact, it was the first thing I thought about upon waking. I was excited to be learning about God and most of all being with God. I could feel Him sitting on the bed with me as I poured over every Word. I was involved in several mail Bible Studies which always led me down other paths, I believed God wanted me to walk with Him.

God was not only leading me in the Bible, He was leading me to books that He wanted me to read in order to expand on who He was. I am so grateful to Joseph Prince Ministries, Joyce Meyer Ministries, Max Lucado Ministries, Rabbi Schneider Ministries and many others who donated their books to those of us in prison. They are doing tremendous work in God's Kingdom. God has blessed them so that they could bless others, including me.

One way for me to more fully understand God, He led me to explore more deeply whatever I was needing in my life, day to day. I had acquired a black and white journaling book and was quickly filling it up. I started with scriptures that dealt with being attacked by the enemy. My first entries were under the caption; Oh Hear Me, were:

> *But God, who is rich in mercy, because of His great love with which He loved us, even when we were dead in trespasses, made us alive together with Christ (by grace you have been saved), and raised us up together, and made us sit together in the heavenly places in Christ Jesus, that in the ages to come He might show the exceeding riches of His grace in His kindness toward us in Christ Jesus.*
> **- Ephesians 2:4-7**

A Plea for Deliverance and Forgiveness; *Psalm* of David.

> *To You, O LORD, I lift up my soul. O my God, I trust in You; Let me not be ashamed; Let not my enemies triumph over me. Indeed, let no one who waits on You be ashamed; Let those be ashamed who deal treacherously without cause.*
> **- Psalm 25:1-3**

One thing you have plenty of in prison, is time and I was plagued daily with what had happened to me and those I felt were responsible for putting me there. I had never been a revengeful person, but I wanted justice and I wanted the truthful story to come out. At the same time I was begging God to take this burden from me. It was like a heavy lead blanket laying over me and at times I could barely breathe.

Prayer and Praise for Deliverance from Enemies; A Meditation of David, which he sang to the LORD

> *O LORD my God, in You I put my trust; Save me from all those who persecute me; And deliver me, Lest they tear me like a lion, Rending me in pieces, while there is none to deliver.*

> *O LORD my God, if I have done this: If there is iniquity in my hands, If I have repaid evil to him who was at peace with me, Or have plundered my enemy without cause, Let the enemy pursue me and overtake me; Yes, let him trample my life to the earth, And lay my honor in the dust. Selah*
> **- Psalm 7:1-5**

Not only was I focusing on who had been a part of this downfall, in addition to that, all of the liars and outright sociopaths who wanted me behind bars, but I agonized over my lack of discernment to see what was really going on. How could I have been so stupid? So many dear friends had been dreadfully harmed and they had trusted me to steer them into the right direction. I hated myself for being a tool of destruction. To say that I was haunted daily would be an apt description. My mind was in turmoil and the only time I found peace was when I was with God in His Word.

Another fear that plagued me was how I was going to be treated after I was released. I couldn't even imagine how that would be. By this time, I knew who my real friends were, they were still beside me and always there to lift me up. I was saddened with a few women that had dropped me like a hot potato, allowing me to see that they never were true friends in the first place. Bigger still, was how was my family going to react? So many questions, so many unanswered questions.

Spending more and more time in the Word was the only way that I could breathe, lower anxiety and basically stay centered. It became clear to me that God was my defender, that He alone could and would surround me with His angels for comfort and kindness, both of which were non-existent behind the barbed wire.

> *Turn Yourself to me, and have mercy on me, For I am desolate and afflicted. The troubles of my heart have enlarged; Bring me out of my distresses!*
>
> *Look on my affliction and my pain, And forgive all my sins. Consider my enemies, for they are many; And they hate me with cruel hatred.*

Keep my soul, and deliver me; Let me not be ashamed, for I put my trust in You. Let integrity and uprightness preserve me, For I wait for You.
- **Psalm 25:16-21**

Be merciful to me, O God, be merciful to me! For my soul trusts in You; And in the shadow of Your wings I will make my refuge, Until these calamities have passed by.
- **Psalm 57:1**

Though I walk in the midst of trouble, You will revive me; You will stretch out Your hand Against the wrath of my enemies, And Your right hand will save me.
- **Psalm 138:7**

Fear not, for I am with you; Be not dismayed, for I am your God. I will strengthen you, Yes, I will help you, I will uphold you with My righteous right hand.'
- **Isaiah 41:10**

There was no doubt then or now that God was directing me to His Words of comfort and strength and encouragement. He knew exactly what I needed and He was delivering it in ways that I could understand. I could feel it, I believed it. I had always dreamed of having a closer relationship with Him and here, day by day we were walking together.

I have found that the trials of life are like precious stones, sparkling, calling to me to pay attention, something great is about to happen. Instead of fearing the darkness that we all find in our lives from time to time, have faith that something great is about to happen ... Change is coming

The greater the darkness, the brighter the light when you make it through the storm. It is at this time that deep lessons can be learned that will strengthen our faith or lead us to our Lord Jesus Christ. We must embrace the life jacket that God will provide for us ... Change is coming.

Eventually the turbulence will pass, it will not last forever. I have found that in those times, God is polishing me so that I can sparkle and become more of the daughter that He created.

CHAPTER 17

LIVING IN THE LIGHT

I will bring the blind by a way they did not know; I will lead them in paths they have not known. I will make darkness light before them, And crooked places straight. These things I will do for them, And not forsake them.
- Isaiah 42:16

Truly the light is sweet, And it is pleasant for the eyes to behold the sun; But if a man lives many years And rejoices in them all, Yet let him remember the days of darkness, For they will be many. All that is coming is vanity.
- Ecclesiastes 11:7-8

God was becoming a bigger and bigger part of my days and thoughts and I could feel His Presence. I wasn't lonely, I was loved, and prison life was becoming more and more just a blur, the days just melting away.

God was directing my path, leading me through scripture to heal the very broken Mary. He knew my life's story, He knew me before I was conceived, and He alone knew exactly what I needed. I am grateful today that I turned to God and not anything or anyone else to soothe the pain, to soothe the longing in my soul, to fill up the emptiness.

> *Be gracious to me, O Lord, For to You I cry all day long. Make glad the soul of Your servant, For to You, O Lord, I lift up my soul. For You, Lord, are good, and ready to forgive, And abundant in lovingkindness to all who call upon You.*
> **- Psalm 86:3-5**

> *Do not fear, for I am with you; Do not anxiously look about you, for I am your God. I will strengthen you, surely I will help you, Surely I will uphold you with My righteous right hand.*
> **- Isaiah 41:10**

> *Though I walk in the midst of trouble, You will revive me; You will stretch forth Your hand against the wrath of my enemies, And Your right hand will save me.*
> **- Psalm 138:7**

I was still doing several mail Bible studies, most of them centering on John. One day, I asked God to fill me with His Light, I wanted it to illuminate my path and fill me up so that I could be a light to others. In the silence He told me to search His Word for the word light and write that verse down, in doing so, I would come to understand Him further. It is from that notebook that I am writing the rest of the most amazing journey with God. The Word was God Himself talking to me and I was reading scripture that I had read before, but now, it is as if He wrote it just for me!

Spring was finally showing herself on the campus of the facility. The flowers were blooming and the birds were singing. I actually was enjoying God's gift of nature again. As I passed other inmates coming and going, it looked like they were oblivious to their surroundings.

Due to a shortage of P.O.A.'s and higher numbers of inmates that needed to be watched, I was working more and more. I had switched from a morning shift to an afternoon shift, working with a new group of fellow P.O.A.'s. There were times that my soul was jarred from what I saw and heard and usually when my shift was done, I would go back to my cell and just crash. My bunk was placed directly in front of a long south facing window and the sunlight warmed me and soothed me to sleep. God's light was everywhere!

> *Truly the light is sweet, And it is pleasant for the eyes to behold the sun; But if a man lives many years And rejoices in them all, Yet let him remember the days of darkness, For they will be many. All that is coming is vanity.*
> - **Ecclesiastes 11:7-8**

> *The sun shall no longer be your light by day, Nor for brightness shall the moon give light to you; But the LORD will be to you an everlasting light, And your God your glory. Your sun shall no longer go down, Nor shall your moon withdraw itself; For the LORD will be your everlasting light, And the days of your mourning shall be ended.*
> - **Isaiah 60:19-20**

I felt like God's light was filling my body with healing energy. My mental and physical body were becoming stronger and stronger. I was walking faster and faster and my energy level wasn't being zapped with each step. I also noticed that my breathing was becoming easier as well. I definitely was not the same person I was, inside and out, as when I arrived here that crisp spring morning a year ago.

Back then, my mind and body had shut down and everything was a huge use of energy just to move and think. I had always heard of the mind-body connection and I was witnessing it firsthand. I was amazed that God's light had done this for me.

It was about this time that God must have decided I was ready for Jesus. I grew up knowing that Jesus was love and that he had died and risen again. Somewhere on the journey, I had decided that I didn't need Jesus, I didn't need anyone to intercede for me! I had a special connection to God and I just went straight to the "Big Guy" with everything. I actually had the nerve to tell my pastor at the time that very thing. She was aghast of course and just told me not to rule Jesus out altogether. Thinking about it today, I can't even imagine what she thought.

I remember being on a church committee that was writing the church's mission statement. I created quite a stir insisting that we be a God focused church, not a Christ centered church.

I actually was quite mad at a man that wouldn't back down and in the end, it was voted that we were a Christ centered church . . . Thank God!

During my Bible study of John, it was obvious that Jesus was the central theme of the gospel, however, I wasn't putting it together that I NEEDED JESUS. Because our Father loved me so much, He was going to correct me as any good parent would do. I was clueless where this was all going.

> *For it is the God who commanded light to shine out of darkness, who has shone in our hearts to give the light of the knowledge of the glory of God in the face of Jesus Christ.*
> **- 2 Corinthians 4:6**

> *But if we walk in the light as He is in the light, we have fellowship with one another, and the blood of Jesus Christ His Son cleanses us from all sin.*
> **- 1 John 1:7**

> *I have come as a light into the world, that whoever believes in Me should not abide in darkness.*
> **- John 12:46**

> *Then Jesus spoke to them again, saying, "I am the light of the world. He who follows Me shall not walk in darkness, but have the light of life."*
> **- John 8:12**

Yes indeed, God was going to correct my 'stinkin thinkin' in a loving and patient way that only a Father could do. Isn't God Great! Amen! We started quite a dialog about Jesus which meant that God was going to educate me about who He, God really was. I knew the mechanics of God, but I didn't know God. I was excited about my time in God's word. Think about it, I was being schooled by God himself! Imagine that!

I needed to re-adjust my attitude, I needed to fully embrace that is wasn't all about me. If going to prison didn't do it, I don't know what would have. I was beginning to see how the Father had orchestrated everything so that it would all come together, just for me.

CHAPTER 18

The Power Of Three

However, when He, the Spirit of truth, has come, He will guide you into all truth; for He will not speak on His own authority, but whatever He hears He will speak; and He will tell you things to come.
- John 16:13

The grace of the Lord Jesus Christ, and the love of God, and the communion of the Holy Spirit be with you all. Amen.
- 2 Corinthians 13:14

God is so Awesome! God knew that I knew and believed in the Trinity, but He also knew it was a difficult concept for many people to understand. God is three parts, The Father, The Son and The Holy Ghost, which is sometimes called The Spirit of Truth, Comforter, The Witness and Living Waters.

Looking back at my life, I finally put it together, that the visitation that I received when I was eleven was God, in Jesus, bestowing on me The Holy Spirit. He told me I would never be alone and I wasn't. There were times in my life that I heard that small voice and most of those times I ignored it. To say I was head strong is a mild way of describing me. I think my challenging everything was a great coping mechanism for the time, but there did come a day that it no longer served me, for example, being in prison. To be head strong in prison is not a good choice, not at all.

Every day in the morning before I went to work, I had my coffee in the day room and sat with other women who were focused on God and some that were learning about God. I always shared with them where I was at on my journey. I know in discussing the Holy Ghost that for many, it was hard for them to comprehend.

The exciting thing is that they wanted to know how to "get" the Holy Spirit. Since I now believed that I had received the spirit when I was eleven, I didn't have the answer. As you probably can guess, that was the first question I asked God the next day. His answer was the same, look for it in the Word. I share these scriptures with you because that is exactly how God answered me. God's Word is God. That is one of the ways that we communicate. I love God, I love the Word.

The Certainty of God's Witness

This is He who came by water and blood—Jesus Christ; not only by water, but by water and blood. And it is the Spirit who bears witness, because the Spirit is truth. For there are three that bear witness in heaven: the Father, the Word, and the Holy Spirit; and these three are one.
- 1 John 5:6-7

The Spirit of the LORD shall rest upon Him, The Spirit of wisdom and understanding, The Spirit of counsel and might, The Spirit of knowledge and of the fear of the LORD.
- Isaiah 11:2

Nevertheless I tell you the truth. It is to your advantage that I go away; for if I do not go away, the Comforter will not come to you; but if I depart, I will send Him to you. And when He has come, He will convict the world of sin, and of righteousness, and of judgment:

- John 16:7-8

And when they had prayed, the place where they were assembled together was shaken; and they were all filled with the Holy Spirit, and they spoke the word of God with boldness.
- Acts 4:31

I grasped the concept of how the Apostles had received The Holy Spirit, however, how do we receive it?

I had always had a thirst for knowledge and it was like I was on a mission to find the answers that my soul was asking. God is very direct, He doesn't beat around the bush, if you are seeking something, and you will find it. I was not only finding the knowledge that I needed but the wisdom on how to use the knowledge. I felt God was preparing me for the journey ahead, a journey that He had planned, a journey that I would gladly follow anywhere.

It was an exciting time to be sure, but it was also a time like no other. I don't ever remember asking God for direction, after all, I was going to do it my way, anyways. I had been such a brat, I wonder how God could even have withstood me.

While I was looking for knowledge of the Holy Ghost, I kept running across being saved or born again. They were terms I had heard, however, they were not terms that any of the churches I attended used. God was opening new concepts that were going to blow my mind. Each day brought me closer, I wasn't sure what that was, but I could feel it. It was almost as if God was excited about it as I was.

And I will pray the Father, and He will give you another-Helper, that He may abide with you forever— the Spirit of Truth, whom the world cannot receive, because it neither sees Him nor knows Him; but you know Him, for He dwells with you and will be in you.
- John 14:16-17

Or do you not know that your body is the temple of the Holy Spirit who is in you, whom you have from God, and you are not your own?

- 1 Corinthians 6:19

Jesus answered, "Most assuredly, I say to you, unless one is born of water and the Spirit, he cannot enter the kingdom of God. That which is born of the flesh is flesh, and that which is born of the Spirit is spirit. Do not marvel that I said to you, 'You must be born again.' The wind blows where it wishes, and you hear the sound of it, but cannot tell where it comes from and where it goes. So is everyone who is born of the Spirit."
- John 3:5-8

So, there it was, I needed to be born of water, which I interpreted as being baptized and born of the Spirit. I knew I had the Spirit since all those years ago when God had visited me and I had been baptized by the sprinkling of the water, but I was still missing something . . . what was it?

I was getting impatient with God, I wanted all of the answers now! I had put a lot of effort to get where I was. God, with a good sense of humor, let me know to trust His process and allow Him to transform my life, as it was His plan and would be in His timing. Miracles were happening every day, I needed to take time to enjoy them, ponder them and just rest. The greatest miracle is that in my seeking, He was answering me through His Word. He had me zigzagging all over the Bible.

For thus says the Lord GOD, the Holy One of Israel: "In returning and rest you shall be saved; In quietness and confidence shall be your strength."
- Isaiah 30:15

I waited patiently for the LORD; And He inclined to me, And heard my cry.
- Psalm 40:1

Surely I have calmed and quieted my soul, Like a weaned child with his mother; Like a weaned child is my soul within me.
– Psalm 131:2

As I walked to chow, the med line, and to work, I was constantly in conversation with God. Everyone that I passed, I smiled and said God bless you. For the most part, that brought a smile to their face, some said Amen and a few just ignored me.

CHAPTER 19

There Is Only LOVE

But whoever keeps His word, truly the love of God is perfected in him. By this we know that we are in Him.
- 1 John 2:5

I was advancing in my Bible studies of John, which is clearly all about love. I have not known unconditional love here on Earth, however, God is love and love is God. In one of my pity party moments about never being loved, God interrupted me and told me that this way of thinking had to stop. God, in the only way a loving father could, reminded me that He has always loved me, even before I was conceived and has never stopped loving and adoring me, so quit whining about not being loved. Don't you just love God's sense of humor?

As I sat there pondering all that He had said, I realized that I didn't know love and if I didn't know love, I didn't know the fullness of God. After a few moments, I asked God to show me love and of course, that led to scriptures dealing with love.

Scripture dealing with love is everywhere in the Bible, in fact, I think it is a love story of just how much God does love us. Love is a strong emotion, but I was beginning to see that there was more to love than that. So many of us put love in a box and label it "Romantic Love."

In my King James Version of the Bible, I found that charity was used instead of love. For example:

> *Though I speak with the tongues of men and of angels, and have not charity, I am become as sounding brass, or a tinkling cymbal. And though I have the gift of prophecy, and understand all mysteries, and all knowledge; and though I have all faith, so that I could remove mountains, and have not charity, I am nothing. And though I bestow all my goods to feed the poor, and though I give my body to be burned, and have not charity, it profited me nothing.*
>
> *Charity suffereth long, and is kind; charity envied not; charity vaunted not itself, is not puffed up, Doth not behave itself unseemly, seeketh not her own, is not easily provoked, thinketh no evil; Rejoiced not in iniquity, but rejoiced in the truth; Beareth all things, believeth all things, hoped all things, endured all things.*
>
> *Charity never failed: but whether there be prophecies, they shall fail; whether there be tongues, they shall cease; whether there be knowledge, it shall vanish away. For we know in part, and we prophesy in part. But when that which is perfect is come, then that which is in part shall be done away. When I was a child, I spoke as a child, I understood as a child, I thought as a child: but when I became a man, I put away childish things. For now we see through a glass, darkly; but then face to face: now I know in part; but then shall I know even as also I am known.*
>
> *And now abides faith, hope, charity, these three; but the greatest of these is charity.*
>
> **- 1 Corinthians 13:1-13 (KJV)**

1 Corinthians was written by the apostle Paul to the church he established in Corinth, Greece. I was finding that sometimes, in the translation to English the full "flavor" was

missing and this was just one of those times. In Greek, charity's meaning was *agape* or love and it was defined by verbs (action words) rather than by adjectives (defining words). Why do I think this is important? Because when we say God loves us, we are limiting it to what we define as love. God's love for us is so much more. As I write this I am so blown away by just how much God loves me, what His actions of love towards me are.

So what is the fullness of charity/love? I went to my Henry Morris Study Bible and he gave this for the meaning of the word:

> Charity means a generous and unselfish concern for others in view of the almost universal misuse of the English word "love" today, generally denoting either romantic love or erotic love or possibly just a happy feeling.

> Agape is a Greco-Christian term referring to love, "the highest form of love, charity" and "the love of God for man and of man for God". The word is not to be confused with philia, brotherly love, as it embraces a universal, unconditional love that transcends and persists regardless of circumstance. The noun form first occurs in the Septuagint, but the verb form goes as far back as Homer, translated literally as affection, as in "greet with affection" and "show affection for the dead". Other ancient authors have used forms of the word to denote love of a spouse or family, or affection for a particular activity, in contrast to Eros. – Wikipedia

With this definition, we see in this verse, that without charity, "I am nothing and have nothing." Wow, God LOVE, LOVE, LOVE, LOVES me. Did I tell you God LOVES me? The great news is that He LOVES you too!

It was during this time of understanding how God's love was for me that a softening of heart started. God's love was melting the barriers I had put up so that love couldn't hurt me anymore. I was starting to view myself differently which meant I was viewing my surroundings and the world differently. The most startling difference was how I viewed people. I was starting to see them as God sees and loves them. Wow, just wow.

When you know, really know that you are loved, you view the world differently and you also view yourself differently. There in the middle of prison I was changing and that change would be my salvation. I could have never known what was going to happen, but God did, it was HIS PLAN.

I love the LORD, because He has heard my voice and my supplications.
- **Psalm 116:1**

The LORD your God in your midst, The Mighty One, will save; He will rejoice over you with gladness, He will quiet you with His love, He will rejoice over you with singing."
- **Zephaniah 3:17**

"Therefore you shall love the LORD your God, and keep His charge, His statutes, His judgments, and His commandments always.
- **Deuteronomy 11:1**

Love and Joy Perfected

"As the Father loved Me, I also have loved you; abide in My love. If you keep My commandments, you will abide in My love, just as I have kept My Father's commandments and abide in His love.
- **John 15:9-10**

Obedience by Faith

Whoever believes that Jesus is the Christ is born of God, and everyone who loves Him who begot also loves him who is begotten of Him. By this we know that we love the children of God, when we love God and keep His commandments. For this is the love of God, that we keep His commandments. And His commandments are not burdensome.
- **1 John 5:1-3**

Loving God During Trials

Blessed is the man who endures temptation; for when he has been approved, he will receive the crown of life which the Lord has promised to those who love Him.
- James 1:12

I will give you a new heart and put a new spirit within you; I will take the heart of stone out of your flesh and give you a heart of flesh. I will put My Spirit within you and cause you to walk in My statutes, and you will keep My judgments and do them.
- Ezekiel 36:26-27

For God so loved the world that He gave His only begotten Son, that whoever believes in Him should not perish but have everlasting life.
- John 3:16

While reading more and more about how God loved me and that I should love the Lord, God was sending me to scripture that started to speak of Jesus. Now I remind you that I believed in Jesus, I believed He was God's only begotten son, born of a virgin, I believed all that. But what I didn't believe was that I needed Him to be a mediator between God and I. God and I were having a love-fest and that was good enough for me.

Every day I was led to more scriptures on the love of God, Jesus and being saved and being born again. Now, I was definitely in new territory. The churches that I attended, never brought up any of these concepts. I wondered if it was just the denominations that I attended or had I missed what was being taught, all along. Of course, I had heard the terms born again and saved, in fact I had a friend that claimed she was both. My understanding on the topics was zero. I had plenty to research and I had plenty of time to do it.

I was still doing my P.O.A. job which gave me an opportunity to be out of my cell and unit. I was working about five days a week and lately had been assigned to segregation in the ward in the medical facility. I was stunned to see that my assigned person was none other than the inmate that had cut herself! I knew that she had survived that fateful night that felt like a hundred years ago.

She smiled as I sat down in front of her door and got up and stood across from me. She must have sensed that I was full of questions and knew that out of respect for her, I wouldn't ask. I did ask her what she was doing on this observation wing and evidently, she had tried to kill herself by ingesting glass. I don't know where she got it, but where there is a will, there is a way.

She went on to tell me that this time would be her last time in isolation. She knew that she was going to be there for a long time and with time on her hands, she had started reading the Bible and had started a Bible study. I smiled and told her yes, God was great and was with me every moment of every day. She went on to explain that she was finding new "stuff" and had a lot to think about.

I never question anyone when they start talking about finding God. In prison, there were so many reasons to make that decision. Boredom, getting out to go to the chapel, having something new to talk about and of course, for many, they were able to talk to the C.O.'s about Jesus. I think there actually were a few that felt the pull of the Lord, seeking and searching. There were a lot of religious, spiritual books in the libraries for anyone to find. We had been so blessed that many authors had copies of their books sent in.

I had the opportunity to observe her for several weeks, when one day, when I came in she immediately told me not to talk to her. Evidently, she and her therapist were not seeing eye-to-eye on the continuation of her treatment and the length of time she was going to stay on this floor. She was angry, she wanted a new therapist and was making everyone on the hall aware of it. When one of the prisoners were acting out, the whole hall felt that they should too. It was a total zoo.

It would be several months before I would see her again, this time in her assigned unit, while I was observing someone else. She said she was doing better and seemed happier. I don't know what her diagnosis was, but I did know she had violent mood swings and didn't want to take medication that made her feel like a 'zombie,' as she put it. Remember, her treatment plan was all about managing her while she was in prison, not actually any treatment that would help her.

I had plenty of time to ponder God, His Word and Jesus when I was on duty. For many of the people that I observed, they were medicated so that they would sleep most of the time.

I loved God so much, I beginning to understand just how disobedient I had been. I had never surrendered to God or His "way." My ego was fighting to stay in control, there was a real battle going on inside of me, I could feel it.

I actually felt so agitated that I realized something had to give. I didn't know what, but it had better happen soon. With all that I had to put up with prison life, I certainly didn't need to have this internal war going on.

My prayer life was going well, I actually could focus on my family, friends and of course my past clients. Through my Bible studies I was learning to pray for myself. Odd as it sounds, I never had asked God for things or to intercede for me. I always prayed for other people, not myself. It was at this time that I found The Prayer of Jabez by Bruce Wilkinson. It is a small book and I devoured it. I really had never read Chronicles, where the prayer of Jabez is located, it was so boring and was all about the lineage of the people in the Old Testament. But tucked away was this beautiful prayer. I said it every day and still do.

> *And Jabez called on the God of Israel saying, "Oh, that You would bless me indeed, and enlarge my territory, that Your hand would be with me, and that You would keep me from evil, that I may not cause pain!" So God granted him what he requested.*
> **- 1 Chronicles 4:10**

I came to the realization that the reason that I never prayed for myself or asked God for anything is that I didn't believe that I was worthy to ask. I had learned early in life that I didn't matter, not really. So if you don't matter, no need to waste God's time asking Him for anything, He had better things to do and people that mattered to care about.

I let God know that I was curious about being saved, being born again and it was as if He couldn't wait to show me.

> *"For the Son of Man has come to seek and to save that which was lost."*
> **- Luke 19:10**

> *For God sent not his Son into the world to condemn the world; but that the world through him might be saved.*
> **- John 3:17**

> *And this I pray, that your love may abound yet more and more in knowledge and in all judgment; That you may approve things that are excellent; that you may be sincere and without offence till the day of Christ. Being filled with the fruits of*

righteousness, which are by Jesus Christ, unto the glory and praise of God.
-Philippians 1:9-11

A new heart also will I give you, and a new spirit will I put within you: and I will take away the stony heart out of your flesh, and I will give you a heart of flesh. And I will put my spirit within you, and cause you to walk in my statutes, and ye shall keep my judgments, and do them.
- Ezekiel 36:26-27

For we are to God the fragrance of Christ among those who are being saved and among those who are perishing.
- 2 Corinthians 2:15

As I walked around the prison, doing my routine, during the times standing in line, I was pondering all that I had read over and over again. Looking back, I can see where I was isolating myself in order to spend more time with God. I was always friendly and had a smile on my face and a ready word of encouragement, however, I was definitely focused on God's Word.

I found such comfort in focusing on God and yes, Jesus, sweet Jesus. The audacity of me cutting Christ out of my life. I could feel His love for me, how different my life would have been if I had stayed Christ centered.

I was really taking a hard look at my entire life and I didn't like what I saw. In not surrendering to God and not placing Christ at the center of my heart, I did it my way, as Frank Sinatra once sang. At the time, I was proud that I had did 'it' my way, never once asking God what His plan was for me. I was pure EGO, which separated me from God.

I was so ashamed, saddened and wondered what I could do to make this right. I knew that God loved me, and Christ was rooting for me and in some way, I knew that the answer to my question would be answered in the Word. In acknowledging that God was in control and if I surrendered it all to Him, I would find my salvation.

One of my cell mates told me that all I did was talk about God and she was tired of hearing it. I remember having a smirky smile on my face, knowing that I wasn't going to stop. This same inmate had told me to never hum while she was in the cell, which was all of the time. Up to this point I had tried to adhere to her demand just to have peace in the room, but something was changing inside of me and I didn't know if I could continue to honor that.

> *Therefore He is also able to save to the uttermost those who come to God through Him, since He always lives to make intercession for them.*
> **- Hebrews 7:25**

> *So they said, "Believe on the Lord Jesus Christ, and you will be saved, you and your household."*
> **- Acts 16:31**

CHAPTER 20

CONVICTED

Take Up the Cross and Follow Him

Then He said to them all, "If anyone desires to come after Me, let him deny himself, and take up his cross daily, and follow Me. For whoever desires to save his life will lose it, but whoever loses his life for My sake will save it. For what profit is it to a man if he gains the whole world, and is himself destroyed or lost?
- Luke 9:23-25

I went through the Unit's small library at least a couple of times a week. A book about Heaven caught my eye. It was "A Divine Revelation of Heaven" by Mary K. Baxter. I found it interesting, however one section really caught my attention, the chapter of being born again and the relationship with Jesus that was so important and without it, you couldn't be saved. There it was again, SAVED.

I had a few other books that I was reading, but the Bible was always my main reading. I felt like God and I were in a discussion and I actually was listening and not trying to lead the way. (That was a first)

It was a day like all the other days, each day running seamless into the next. There was no way that I could have predicted what was going to happen. The scriptures that God had laid out for me were definitely a clear path about was going to happen.

> *Heal me, O LORD, and I shall be healed; Save me, and I shall be saved, For You are my praise.*
> **- Jeremiah 17:14**

> *Being confident of this very thing, that He who has begun a good work in you will complete it until the day of Jesus Christ;*
> *And this I pray, that your love may abound still more and more in knowledge and all discernment, that you may approve the things that are excellent, that you may be sincere and without offense till the day of Christ, being filled with the fruits of righteousness which are by Jesus Christ, to the glory and praise of God.*
> **- Philippians 1:6, 9-11**

> *Therefore He is also able to save to the uttermost those who come to God through Him, since He always lives to make intercession for them.*
> **- Hebrews 7:25**

And here it is, the scripture that convicted me. As I read it, I was so filled with remorse, I was overcome with emotion, the world seemed to have stopped, I wasn't aware of anything happening around me, where I was or even if anyone else was in the cell. I was in the moment and Jesus was there, holding my hand, letting me feel and experience the full measure of the scripture. It was as if time had ceased to exist.

DO NOT LOVE THE WORLD

> *Do not love the world or the things in the world. If anyone loves the world, the love of the Father is not in him. For all that*

is in the world —the lust of the flesh, the lust of the eyes, and the pride of life is not of the Father but is of the world. And the world is passing away, and the lust of it; but he who does the will of God abides forever.
- 1 John 2:15-17

It was all there, laid open. I felt like I was in surgery and had a long incision with all of my innards laying in trays along side of me. I no longer could hide any of my sin, I couldn't even if I had wanted to. The guilt, the shame, the ugliness of it all. While gasping for air and softly saying forgive me, forgive me, forgive me, I was taken further into my earthly self, hating every second of it and sickened by what I saw and felt. I was aware of sweet Jesus still holding my hand as I lamented my life.

I immediately wrote in my journal what was happening and that is what I am conveying to you now. Processing what was going on was the only thing that mattered to me.

LUST of the flesh (Body)	**EARTHLY** victory over **SELF-CONTROL**
LUST of the eyes (Soul)	**SENSUAL** victory over **COVETOUSNESS**
PRIDE of life (Spirit)	**DEVILISH victory over PRIDE**

Again, stating it differently:

SIN . . . Gluttony, Covetousness . . . **CONVICTED!**

SIN . . . Lust, Sexual Pleasures . . . **CONVICTED!**

SIN . . . Pride/Ego . . . **CONVICTED!**

I felt completely naked in front of God and was so ashamed to know that Jesus knew every detail, even before I acknowledged it. This was my true crime, this was my true **CONVICTION**.

If we say that we have no sin, we deceive ourselves, and the truth is not in us. If we confess our sins, He is faithful and just to forgive us our sins and to cleanse us from all unrighteousness.

If we say that we have not sinned, we make Him a liar, and His word is not in us.
- 1 John 1:8-10

This wisdom does not descend from above, but is earthly, sensual, and demonic. For where envy and self-seeking exist, confusion and every evil thing are there.
- James 3:15-16

CHAPTER 21

Forgiven, Saved And Born Again

. . . that if you confess with your mouth the Lord Jesus and believe in your heart that God has raised Him from the dead, you will be saved.
- Romans 10:9

Grace to you and peace from God the Father and our Lord Jesus Christ, who gave Himself for our sins, that He might deliver us from this present evil age, according to the will of our God and Father, to whom be glory forever and ever. Amen.
- Galatians 1:3-5

As I sat there, I felt like there was a tornado swirling around inside of me. It was like all of my sins were in the vortex, not one of them were hidden. I felt the weight of my actions/inactions weighing so heavy on my soul, I was having trouble breathing. How could I go forward with all of this on my conscience?

The Word, I had to focus on the Word, it was calling to me. As I tried to focus on all that I had read for the last year it became crystal clear what I had to do. God had led me to this very moment, He was standing beside me at the foot of the cross, the cross that my Savior, Jesus Christ, had died on for my sins. Sobbing, I knew what I had to do; I had to acknowledge all of these sins, swirling about, to Christ and only He could forgive me. Christ had died for those sins, He had suffered, He felt the pain of not only what was happening to Him physically, but the weight of my sins were with Him.

How could I have been so stupid to think that I didn't need Jesus to have a conversation with God? My biggest sin, PRIDE, and that was the reason. My pride had led me to live my life for me, not God. Anyone who had known me for the past twenty-five years could tell you, it was either my way or the highway.

In asking Jesus to forgive me, I acknowledged that He was the son of God and was the sacrificial lamb for me, giving His life so that I could have mine. I acknowledged that He arose from the dead, three days later and is sitting on the right hand of God. I acknowledged my love for Him and my desire to live a Christ centered life.

The swirling stopped in that instant and in that instant I felt the warmth of Christ's love surrounding me, forgiving me and accepting me into the family of God. I was now His and there would be no one or anything that could separate us.

I felt the change, the old had died and the new was reborn. Yes, I felt it! I was forever changed in that moment. I knew that Jesus would be with me for the rest of my life. I knew that troubles would always find their way to me and in those times I would praise Him, pulling even closer to me. I was His!

I was forgiven, I was born again in Christ and would have an eternal life in Heaven. It doesn't get any better than that. Wow, it still gives me goosebumps. Some people have told me that they didn't feel anything when they were saved, they just knew they were saved. I know just how blessed I am to have had such a "Come to Jesus moment."

The spirit of forgiveness is such a blessing and God our Father sets the example all of us can live by. To think, that I, Mary Faher was forgiven, not only forgiven, but my sins were forgotten by God! Forgiveness is grace, a free gift to all of us who neither deserve it nor in any way can earn it!

> *"I, even I, am He who blots out your transgressions for My own sake; And I will not remember your sins.*
> **- Isaiah 43:25**

> *And be kind to one another, tenderhearted, forgiving one another, even as God in Christ forgave you.*
> **- Ephesians 4:32**

Not only were my sins forgiven, but in that moment I was able to forgive anyone who had ever harmed me, lied to me, and most of all, were all the people that had me imprisoned due to their own agendas. For the last year, I had been like so many felons, thinking about when I got out, what revenge I could take to exact justice. That weight had been lifted and was gone too. God had assured me that if anyone harmed His daughter, they would pay a price, a price that He would exact.

> *Beloved, do not avenge yourselves, but rather give place to wrath; for it is written, "Vengeance is Mine, I will repay," says the Lord.*
> **- Romans 12:19**

> *But I say to you, love your enemies, bless those who curse you, do good to those who hate you, and pray for those who spitefully use you and persecute you.*
> **- Matthew 5:44**

Everything was different after that day. My eyes were seeing such a beautiful pallet of colors and I could see God's artistry in everything He had made. My ears were attuned to the sounds of nature as if it was a song to me. Each person I met, I recognized as a creation of God.

One of the biggest differences was that while in the Word, I felt like I had a better understanding of the scriptures. It was so much clearer to me. Yes, there where mysteries that I didn't understand and I still don't. I came to realize that I was in the infant stage of a born-again, I had so much to learn and by the grace of God, I was given the time.

> *I have been crucified with Christ; it is no longer I who live, but Christ lives in me; and the life which I now live in the flesh I live by faith in the Son of God, who loved me and gave Himself for me.*
> **- Galatians 2:20**

Likewise you also, reckon yourselves to be dead indeed to sin, but alive to God in Christ Jesus our Lord.
- Romans 6:11

Grace to you and peace from God the Father and our Lord Jesus Christ, who gave Himself for our sins, that He might deliver us from this present evil age, according to the will of our God and Father, to whom be glory forever and ever. Amen.
- Galatians 1:3-5

I was so foolish and ignorant; I was like a beast before You. Nevertheless I am continually with You; You hold me by my right hand. You will guide me with Your counsel, And afterward receive me to glory.
Whom have I in heaven but You? And there is none upon earth that I desire besides You. My flesh and my heart fail; But God is the strength of my heart and my portion forever.
- Psalm 73:22-26

He who has the Son has life; he who does not have the Son of God does not have life. These things I have written to you who believe in the name of the Son of God, that you may know that you have eternal life, and that you may continue to believe in the name of the Son of God.
- 1 John 5:12-13

The Command to Love

Behold what manner of love the Father has bestowed on us, that we should be called children of God! Therefore the world does not know us, because it did not know Him. Beloved, now we are children of God; and it has not yet been revealed what

we shall be, but we know that when He is revealed, we shall be like Him, for we shall see Him as He is. And everyone who has this hope in Him purifies himself, just as He is pure.
- 1 John 3:1-3

In re-reading those passages I am just amazed. I wrote exactly what passages that God had led me to at that time. In fact, all of the scripture that I have added was directed by God! I had no idea at the time just how He was going to put this all together. It has only been with my faith that He had already written the book, that I didn't add any great scripture that I would have picked out myself.

In addition to that, each book that found its way to me or me to it was God directed. Wow, still amazed!

I had mentioned earlier one of those books, "A Divine Revelation of Heaven" by Mary K. Baxter. In that book, I had written down the prayer that she had given to be used when someone wanted to be saved. I am beginning to see that even everything that I had written down while I was in prison was directed by God and even more amazing is that I listened and actually did it. God was patiently teaching me about obedience.

Father, in the name of Jesus Christ, I come to you, just as I am. I am a sinner, Lord I have sinned against you and against Heaven. I ask You, Lord Jesus, to forgive me and to come into my heart and save my soul. Let me be born again by the spirit of the Living God.

I give my life to you, Lord Jesus. I believe You are Jesus Christ who was sent to save by soul from Hell. I give You my thanks and praise and honor for redeeming me by Your precious blood.

If you have prayed this prayer and really believed what you prayed, you are now saved. You have asked Jesus Christ into your heart. Begin to confess Him with your lips and praise Him.

To God Be All Praise and Honor.

Mary K. Baxter
"A Divine Revelation of Heaven"

PRAYER

O Lord, live in me. May Your love beat in and through my heart. May You speak through my voice. Jesus, be the strength of my soul and the fire that purges wrongs from my desires. Fill me with Your great abounding grace. In Jesus' name, Amen.
– Unknown Author

But God, who is rich in mercy, for his great love wherewith he loved us, Even when we were dead in sins, hath quickened us together with Christ, (by grace ye are saved;)
For by grace are ye saved through faith; and that not of yourselves: it is the gift of God:
- Ephesians 2:4-5, 8 KJV

Character of the New Man

Therefore, as the elect of God, holy and beloved, put on tender mercies, kindness, humility, meekness, longsuffering;
- Colossians 3:12

Giving thanks unto the Father, which hath made us meet to be partakers of the inheritance of the saints in light: Who hath delivered us from the power of darkness, and hath translated us into the kingdom of his dear Son: In whom we have redemption through his blood, even the forgiveness of sins:
- Colossians 1:12-14

> ***Blessed be the God and Father of our Lord Jesus Christ, who hath blessed us with all spiritual blessings in heavenly places in Christ: According as he hath chosen us in him before the foundation of the world, that we should be holy and without blame before him in love: Having predestinated us unto the adoption of children by Jesus Christ to himself, according to the good pleasure of his will, To the praise of the glory of his grace, wherein he hath made us accepted in the beloved.***
> **- Ephesians 1:3-6**

> ***But when the kindness and the love of God our Savior toward man appeared, not by works of righteousness which we have done, but according to His mercy He saved us, through the washing of regeneration and renewing of the Holy Spirit, whom He poured out on us abundantly through Jesus Christ our Savior.***
> **- Titus 3:4-6**

Let me re-cap what happened that day in prison, when I had lost all hope, feeling totally alone even in the midst of the clamor of prison life, I remembered reading <u>Our Daily Bread</u> about the love of Jesus Christ, stopping and knowing that I wasn't alone, God was with me and that in my pride I had totally left our Lord Jesus Christ out of my life. After all I was Mary A. Faher, I didn't need an intermediary to talk with God, thank you very much!

Jesus, my sweet Jesus, how great is your name. He stretched out His hand and enfolded me in His love. I remember sobbing, rocking, holding my knees to my chest, I was loved, I was somebody worthy of love, I was chosen, I was Jesus' own and to say that my life was changed in that instant, would be a huge understatement.

Between the sobs, I asked for forgiveness for my sins, me the sinner. I had let pride rule my life, I let the desires of the flesh totally unleashed and my biggest sin was denying what I knew...Jesus, sweet Jesus, Son of God Almighty had died for my sins, was crucified and arose on that third day...for me! Jesus, the sinless Jesus had died for me.

From that moment on, I was a changed person. The "old man" was dead, leaving room for the "new man" to be BORN AGAIN. I am now the adopted daughter of our loving Creator...ABBA. My Father who was always there for me in a world that loved me not. I AM LOVED...

GOD WAS CALLING ME TO LIVE A NEW KIND OF LIFE!

CHAPTER 22

CALLED

Therefore, if anyone is in Christ, he is a new creation; old things have passed away; behold, all things have become new. Now all things are of God, who has reconciled us to Himself through Jesus Christ, and has given us the ministry of reconciliation, that is, that God was in Christ reconciling the world to Himself, not imputing their trespasses to them, and has committed to us the word of reconciliation.

Now then, we are ambassadors for Christ, as though God were pleading through us: we implore you on Christ's behalf, be reconciled to God. For He made Him who knew no sin to be sin for us, that we might become the righteousness of God in Him.
- 2 Corinthians 5:17-21

I was born anew! I could feel it, that feeling has not left me. I wondered if I would always feel this way. I sure hoped that it would continue, I was grateful to have hope, joy and peace in my life again. I found that without hope and joy in your life, there was no reason to go on, without them everything was darkness, no light and certainly no love. I think you can survive without peace, however, life with it is magnificent.

I recognized daily that if I hadn't humbled myself in front of Jesus Christ, I would not be experiencing the best days of my life. It sounds odd, doesn't it, that I was smack dab in the middle of prison, living my best life. Who could have thought that possible?

> *But He gives more grace. Therefore He says: "God resists the proud, But gives grace to the humble." Humble yourselves in the sight of the Lord, and He will lift you up.*
> **- James 4:10**

> *Because your heart was tender, and you humbled yourself before the LORD … and you tore your clothes and wept before Me, I also have heard you," says the LORD.*
> **- 2 Kings 22:19**

> *And whoever exalts himself will be humbled, and he who humbles himself will be exalted.*
> **- Matthew 23:12**

My pride had been so over the top that I had missed all of the hope, joy and peace that can only come from the Father, God. I was learning to live in the moment, not looking backwards, which I found that I had a tendency to do. How many of us look back and say if I had only known what I know now, how different things would have been? I couldn't change my past, it was only there to learn from so that this moment could be all that God had planned for me. Living in the moment helped keep me stay focused on God and what I was to do for this day. I knew that it would only be by God's grace that I would wake up tomorrow to live another day in the light of the Lord.

God had a plan for me, and I could not deny it. I was looking at the gifts he had given me and realized that I had been honing those aspects of Christian living all of my life. He was preparing me for the life and the calling He would give to me. He gave me a brilliant mind, to always seek more knowledge, now I prayed for the wisdom that came with that knowledge. I didn't fear speaking my mind in front of one or a thousand people. Public speaking was something I enjoyed. I learned that back in high school when I ran for student council and had to give a campaign speech. (My mother said I had been very verbal at a young age, having a large vocabulary.) I remember giving a sermon at church when I was sixteen years old, the topic was: "God is Love." Not only had it been easy for me to speak, it had been easy to write as well.

It all seems so apparent now that God was leading me and I was actually following Him. At some point, I stopped focusing on Him, I stopped letting Him lead, or so I thought, that was the first lie I told myself. I believed it was all about me, very narcissistic, that everything I achieved had been from all of my own efforts. I can testify to you this, I definitely am following God's lead while writing this book.

In fact, during my early hours with God the other day, He let me know that this book wasn't about me, it was about Him! It was about His love and devotion to me and to all of His children. This book is to confirm that He never wants to be separated from any of us. He is patient, however, if He can't get our attention, He will do what it takes to make sure we listen. I can certainly testify to that! And there you have it.

In being born-again, God gave me the "Fruits of the Spirit." It was by His grace, that I received them. A free gift!

> *But the fruit of the Spirit is love, joy, peace, longsuffering (patience), kindness, goodness, faithfulness, gentleness, self-control. Against such there is no law.*
> **- Galatians 5:22-23**

> *For you were once darkness, but now you are light in the Lord. Walk as children of light (for the fruit of the Spirit is in all goodness, righteousness, and truth), finding out what is acceptable to the Lord.*
> **- Ephesians 5:8-10**

I have always known that God had something specific that He wanted me to do. For years, for over forty years, I have had dreams where I was leading a group of people to safety. It could be from a tornado, it could have been from an invading army or even aliens, I was always doing the same thing, helping to save them. In the dreams I could feel the urgency to act, to step up and do what it would take to lead them to a place of refuge. It usually ended the same way, I was always trying to shut the door, struggling against the wind to keep the danger from entering and causing harm to anyone inside.

I asked God what was it that He had planned for me, I let Him know I was eagerly waiting for His response. The one thing I had found was that the Lord does answer prayer, however His timing usually was not my timing. I needed to be obedient, to be still, continue to study the Word and continue with my prayer life. I was confident that with each new scripture I read and studied, God would lead me where I was to go.

> *Brethren, I do not count myself to have apprehended; but one thing I do, forgetting those things which are behind and reaching forward to those things which are ahead, I press toward the goal for the prize of the upward call of God in Christ Jesus.*
> **- Philippians 3:13-14**

> *Who has saved us and called us with a holy calling, not according to our works, but according to His own purpose and grace which was given to us in Christ Jesus before time began.*
> **- 2 Timothy 1:9**

> *For to this you were called, because Christ also suffered for us, leaving us an example, that you should follow His steps:*
> **- Peter 2:21**

I continued with my daily Bible studies, prayers and to be the Light that God had asked me to be. The gift of patience was working, I had always asked for it and now I had a fathomless amount of it. And then, one day, not unlike the rest, I found my calling:

Walk in Unity

> *I, therefore, the prisoner of the Lord, beseech you to walk worthy of the calling with which you were called, with all lowliness and gentleness, with longsuffering, bearing with one another in love, endeavoring to keep the unity of the Spirit in*

the bond of peace. There is one body and one Spirit, just as you were called in one hope of your calling;
- **Ephesians 4:1-4**

I was a child of the Most High and as such, I was called to act like it. Even though I lived in this world, it was not my home. My eternal home is with Jesus Christ and one day He will return for me and all of my brothers and sisters.

While I am here, I am to be an ambassador for Christ, a Light, a beacon for those yet unsaved and most importantly, God had shown me through scripture that I was to embrace my sisters and brothers, lifting them up, loving them and to continue to build on our unity as one body, one spirit in Christ.

So much of the world is counter to all that is holy and in these days, it is difficult for believers to watch as everything seems to be deteriating. It is good to remember that nothing is falling apart, it is all falling into place. God has called not only me, but all of His children to stand in unity, it is the only way we can stay strong, loving and caring. As a believer, we are not required to create unity, we are called to keep the unity that is already ours in Christ Jesus.

The unity is:

- One body, made up of all the believers on Earth.
- One spirit, the spirit who lives in each of the believers.
- One hope, believing in Christ's promise to return and take His followers to Heaven.
- One Lord, Jesus Christ, who by His crucifixion and resurrection, redeemed us by His blood.
- One Faith, for all believers, grounded in the Word.
- One baptism, of the Spirit living within us, being born again.
- One Father, the Heavenly Father of our Lord Jesus Christ.

As I sat there on the bunk, I realized that through the gifts God had given me, whether they were my natural abilities or the spiritual gifts which included the fruits of the Spirit, I would be using all of them to fulfill my calling.

As I pondered the book and all of the journaling I had done, I realized that God had called me to write the book and share it with the world. One word I kept hearing, **Bold**, I was to be bold and transparent in telling my story. Okay, I know, it's God's story.

CHAPTER 23

REJOICE!

Faith Triumphs in Trouble

Therefore, having been justified by faith, we have peace with God through our Lord Jesus Christ, through whom also we have access by faith into this grace in which we stand, and rejoice in hope of the glory of God. And not only that, but we also glory in tribulations, knowing that tribulation produces perseverance; and perseverance, character; and character, hope. Now hope does not disappoint, because the love of God has been poured out in our hearts by the Holy Spirit who was given to us.
- Romans 5:1-5

I was finding it hard to believe that I only had three more months until my earliest parole date, February 9, 2017. Three more months! WOW! It almost seemed to have passed in the blink of an eye.

I was finally feeling what I had witnessed so many other prisoners go through. "Parole Board Panic." At my sentencing, the judge had said that my time would be twenty three months to ten years. When I first arrived here, I never considered the ten years, I was only focused on the twenty three months.

I knew that I had been a model prisoner, I had never even gotten a 'ticket' for an infraction and not many prisoners could say that! Due to the overcrowding, I never was admitted to a vocational class for rehabilitation. I was still on the waiting list for Food Service Tech. I had taken all of the other required courses and should have felt at ease about the whole thing. However, there is always a however, there is so much noise about someone not getting paroled.

I wouldn't say that I was panicking, but my anxiety was definitely on alert. Many prisoners had letters written on their behalf to the Parole Board, stating that they were ready to be released back into society and that, that person was going to assist them when they got out. One inmate had over thirty letters sent in for her. I had zero letters sent in, I didn't feel it was necessary.

Many prisoners have someone come in and do the talking for them. Letting the judge see that there was at least one person who would vouch for their character. I didn't have anyone coming in to talk for me, I had Almighty God standing behind me. I felt I had a secret weapon, Jesus Christ, my defender. I knew that I would have Him standing beside me as I gave my own testimony. I knew that as a faithful believer that I had done what was expected of me and that Jesus had done what was needed to be done behind the scenes. I kept telling myself that there was no reason to panic, that the Lord Almighty was my rock, my defender.

> *The Lord is my rock and my fortress and my deliverer; My God, my strength, in whom I will trust; My shield and the horn of my salvation, my stronghold.*
> **- Psalm 18:2**

> *But the Lord has been my defense, And my God the rock of my refuge.*
> **- Psalm 94:22**

> *The Lord is my strength and song, And He has become my salvation. The voice of rejoicing and salvation Is in the tents of the righteous; The right hand of the Lord does valiantly. The right hand of the Lord is exalted; The right hand of the Lord*

does valiantly. I shall not die, but live, And declare the works
of the LORD. The LORD has chastened-me severely, But He has
not given me over to death.
- **Psalm 118:14-18**

Delight thyself also in the Lord: trust also in Him; and he
shall bring it to pass.
– **Psalm 37:4**

My cellmate had her hearing with the Parole Board and had her father representing her. To say that she had the 'Parole Board Panic' would be an understatement. She had been kicked out of her GED class and had several other infractions to add to her list of her behavior. That morning, she got dressed in her freshly ironed state blues, she curled her hair and put on make-up and off she went.

When my cellmate arrived back at the cell about three hours later, she said everything went fine and that she believed that she got her parole. The board member didn't tell her that, he told her that he would discuss it with the other two on the panel and she would be notified. I learned later that she had lied. She would not be released without a GED. She had already been in the class for over three years and had a tutor and because of her attitude and behavior, it had not progressed very well.

The Parole Board met in the Visitors Center, in one of the back conference rooms. I had envisioned a Table with the panel sitting across from me, however, I learned that there would be only one board member present via video conference.

There is a debate among inmates about whether to tell or not to tell if you got your parole and exactly when that date was. Many felt that if everyone knew, there might be someone who would sabotage that parole by planting bogus 'evidence.' For example, putting drugs under the mattress or a shank (an object shaped into a knife.)

My day finally arrived and while there was some anxiety, my Defender was doing His job of reassuring me and kept me focused on Him and not what was about to happen. I have been so blessed to have blind faith in our God. I love the saying, "Let go, let God." That saying never had as much relevance as it did that day.

I got up early and put on my ironed state blues, brushed my hair and didn't put on any make up. I didn't preen in front of the mirror to see if I looked okay. I just went.

When I arrived at the Visitors Center, I along with about twenty other women were seated and had to wait my turn for the "BIG" event. I sat there, breathing in and out slowly, talking to God.

Finally it was my turn. I was led to the conference room and was told to sit in the chair behind the conference table. I sat there, looking around and was surprised to see the condition of the room. It looked like the décor was from the eighties. A lot of oak and brass and the chairs were padded in a melon color. What struck me as the oddest of all, was the television screen was at the far end of the room and when the parole board member appeared, she seemed so far away, I knew that she probably couldn't see me any better than I could see her. At the time, I remember saying to myself that I was glad that I hadn't put on any makeup or fussed with my hair.

Also at the far end of the room was my unit's ARUM, taking notes on everything that was said. The board member asked me a few questions, the main question being how did I feel about my victims and exactly what was my role in their being financially harmed.

I took a deep sigh, I had prepared for this question knowing that it would be asked. Each of us had been given a booklet at the time we had orientation after we were registered, photographed and dressed in our state issued clothing. Of course, I had thrown my booklet away, thinking that I didn't need it and parole seemed so far away. I had gotten a copy of it from another cellmate that had already been paroled. I just shake my head, arrogant! I had been such a brat, how had God continued to love me when I didn't even love myself?

I explained what had happened, what my role was and how remorseful I was that my client's, my friends and family had been scammed by the owners of the company. That they had trusted me to lead them into sound investments and that I had betrayed that trust. I had let them down, I hadn't done my due diligence and had been conned with them being harmed. She asked me a few other questions, like where did I intend to live and how did I expect to support myself.

And just like that it was over. She told me that she would consult with the other two members on the panel and I would be notified about whether or not I would get my parole. With that, the screen went black and the door opened and I returned to my unit.

I knew that I would be questioned about what had happened and if I thought I had gotten my parole. I felt confident that I did get my parole. It helped that the prison was overcrowded, my bed was needed to accommodate the new women that were dropped off each day.

Of course, there was that small voice that told me not to be so sure. The State of Michigan had been so vengeful that I still had fears that they would try and block my parole. That was untrue, the voice was just noise coming from Satan and I had my Defender working on my behalf. I told Satan to be gone in the name of Jesus Christ!

About a week later, I received my letter from the Parole Board stating I did get my parole and it also listed what conditions that I was to follow while I was on parole, which would be for one year. When I completed my parole, the ten years, the maximum of my sentence would be dropped.

To say that I was breathing easier would be an understatement. It was such a relief and the weight of not knowing was lifted, just like a butterfly soaring to the heavens.

I was so thankful to my Lord and Savior, Jesus Christ!!! I didn't know how I would have survived the darkest time of my life without Him. I would REJOICE and praise His name in darkness and light and give Him the glory for everything.

Be glad in the Lord and rejoice, you righteous; And shout for joy, all you upright in heart!
- **Psalm 32:11**

CHAPTER 24

The Prodigal Daughter

And he arose and came to his father. But when he was still a
great way off, his father saw him and had compassion, and ran
and fell on his neck and kissed him. And the son said to him,
'Father, I have sinned against heaven and in your sight, and
am no longer worthy to be called your son.'
- Luke 15:20-21

With the confirmation of my parole over, my thoughts turned to what I would face when I was released. How could I live with the label of Felon? I knew that shame wasn't of God and that Satan would use that to bring a division between Christ and me. It was a division that I wasn't going to allow. In prayer, I asked for God's grace, to live with humility and the strength to live in His light.

As someone who always said that your word, your integrity would be the mark of who you were. Today, the journey has brought me to understand what I want to be remembered as, a child of the God most High and as the daughter to the King, I loved, I praised and danced in the light.

I needed to stay focused on what I could do, I couldn't control how others would see me or receive me. I already knew there were friends, good friends, which had chosen not to stand by me. At first I was crushed by that, however I now knew that was their path and it actually didn't have anything to do with me, but with them. I prayed for them along with those that had sought to do me harm.

I was grateful that I was living my best life, day to day, that I had been forgiven by God's mercy and grace. In all reality, what is most important, what people think of me or what God thinks of me? That is a no brainer . . .

I was concerned that my health had continued to deteriate. My mobility was still very shaky, which could limit my activities. While my body was in this state, my brain was becoming clearer and I could feel the healing that it needed. I strongly believe that the time I had spent in scripture helped me to focus and remember what I had read. Yes, with God all things are possible.

With only two months to go before I stepped outside of those gates, I was moved, for the final time, to the 'Going Home' unit. It was the unit that my old bunkie back in Harrison had been working on. The building that was converted from a gymnasium to a kitchen/cafeteria into a housing unit, due to the overcrowding.

It was a move that I welcomed! I knew that it brought me closer to going home. Home . . . that was something that I really tried not to focus on. I had been notified by the Crown Prince that there had been an estate sale held, selling everything with the exception of a few things and the house was sold with the State of Michigan taking all of the proceeds.

One of the sins that I had been convicted on was my idol worship of material things. I had surrounded myself with beautiful treasures, they were the company that I kept along with my pets. My home had been my fortress, a place of refuge from a loveless life. My bigger crime was that I never gave thanks to God for any of it. I had did it all on my own. I was certainly living larger than the humble beginnings of my life, I liked to say, "You have come a long way baby."

When my thoughts turned to what I had lost, I grieved. I knew it would be a process, after all, I could now see how God had taken it all away for me, so that I could be free to focus on Him. I also was tested in my forgiving the Crown Prince for not even reading my list of what I wanted saved. I forgave him, however, I felt like I didn't matter to him, he did what was easy for him, not taking into account what I wanted. I had no idea what had been saved and what I would have for the future. I never once considered what all of this had did to him. His mother was in prison!

There was a bright spot and that was the paradise that awaited my return in Florida. I could focus on that and be grateful to God for giving it to me, knowing what I needed. I asked Him to find the right church for me to praise and worship Him along with living in His Word. It had to be a Bible based church, all about Jesus!

After settling into my new unit, I was struck by the noise of the vaulted ceiling and the glaring lights that were turned on early and turned off late. It was the first time that I was housed with very young women who definitely had a different way of acting in close quarters with others. In other words, they talked a lot and were loud.

It felt odd that there were no doors to the rooms, everyone could see what you were doing and you could see what they were doing, even when you didn't want to.

The biggest surprise was that my new bunkie was my first bunkie from Unit 9! She was so happy to see me that I felt like I was coming home. There was only one problem. I bet you guessed it, I had been assigned to the top bunk! I had been down this road before and knew what I had to do. I found my bottom bunk detail and took it over to the C.O. and she told me that I would be re-assigned to the next bottom bunk when one opened up. Until then, I had to stay where I was.

I didn't miss my old unit for anything, this definitely was a step up. No stairs, everything was on one floor. The bathroom was equipped with real toilets, not those cold stainless steel ones. The showers were great, they all had plenty of hot water and the pressure was perfect. The only drawback was that there appeared to be gnats coming out of the drains and sometimes there were terrible odors coming out. I just kept in mind that this too would pass and that freedom wasn't that far away. It is amazing what you can tolerate when you know that it is only for a short time.

We were having fun being together. We shared our love of Jesus every time that we could and boy can that woman praise our Lord, Jesus Christ. She was paroling to Georgia, not going back to Michigan. We both agreed that Michigan is not a felon friendly state. She had a husband and a daughter waiting for her, along with extended family. She was all set to leave about a week before I was.

Wow, it really was like coming home, my Bible giving friend was moved into the unit also, her time to go home had finally arrived. It was so good to see her. She like me, liked to do Bible study early in the morning, so we met in the day area and took turns reading from Our Daily bread, Words of Hope, Jesus Always and of course, the Bible. As much time as I had spent alone in the Word, it was so good to be sharing our love of the Lord together.

I got to know her a little better. I never asked what her parole violation had been, I figured if she wanted me to know, she would tell me. She shared with me that she was worried about going home. She would be going back to the same place she had come from. An area that would test her 'mettle' as she liked to say. She admitted that her anger was something that could go from one to a hundred in a second. We prayed about it asking God to give her patience, give her the strength to resist the temptation to anger and to remain steadfast in walking in God's light. As I write this, I pray that she is able to receive her blessings from God, wherever she is at.

A bed finally opened up with a bottom bunk and it was right next door to the room I was in. That was convenient for my old bunkie and me to meet to go to the chow hall together. The move was quick and easy and hopefully would be my last move.

With the move, I had an opportunity to talk "GOD" to a whole set of new people. My new bunkie in the bunk above me was a Messianic Jew. I found that so interesting and we spent quite a bit of time together. She schooled me on what Bible verses are read at Passover and how there are Jews that Loved Jesus and how there seemed to be a lot of Jews coming to believe that Jesus Christ was the Messiah. Wow, what a gift to learn so much about Gods chosen people.

It was a time to reflect and a time not to get too excited about going home. At this point, everything should have gone smoothly. I had been here long enough to know anything could happen and of course it did.

At the time of my parole hearing, I had told the Parole Board member that I would be paroling to my home in Florida and she acknowledged that. I had repeatedly talked to my former unit's ARUM about paperwork on the matter and she said that the state would be sending me everything I would need. Well, here it was about a month before I was released and I had not received it. It was a little unsettling and I figured I had to take the initiative to find out where I was in the process.

The ARUM put up a paper with twenty slots on it for people to sign up to speak with her and if the slots were filled up, you would have to wait until the next time she would be available. I was able to sign right up, I had my morning coffee and sat in the day room until she put the paper up so that I could be near the front of the line. I admit, I didn't walk too fast and it was amazing how the younger women rushed in front of me, cutting in line.

In speaking with the ARUM, she said she would talk to the man that had been assigned as my parole agent in Benton Harbor Michigan and find out where they were on the Out of State Transfer paperwork. I would have to wait until she was available again to find out.

I had an uneasy feeling about it. I didn't trust the State of Michigan to do anything that would be helpful to me. I admit, when it comes to the Michigan legal system, I was a little paranoid, okay, a lot paranoid.

I finally put in my resignation for my P.O.A. position which freed up a lot of time for me. It was just another chapter of prison life that was now closed. There definitely was a feeling of closure with each step that I had to go through before being released. The left hand definitely didn't know what the right hand was doing. MDOC was so inept, they had me going all over the campus, doing things that I had already did. It was a waste of their time and mine.

I had to go to the Education Building and speak with the Dean about my paperwork for my GED or lack of it. I had to again, show her my confirmed record of graduating from High School, adding that I had a B.S. degree as well, therefore, I had not needed a GED. She had me sign a form and I was on my way.

I was so glad that one of the gifts of the Spirit was patience, I needed plenty of it. Even as all of this was unfolding, I could feel the peace that by the grace of God I had received, I don't know how I could have endured this particular phase of going home.

It was a time of reflection for me. I was still doing Bible studies, still pouring over the Word and praying. I knew that God would use this time for my good, at some point. When I thought about that, I always thanked Him for giving me time to come to Jesus, be born-again, to start my life over, living in His light and love.

I was reminded of the parable in the Bible called, **The Parable of the Lost Son**, in Luke 15:11-32. I was the lost daughter! I had in effect told my Father that I would take His blessings and go on to live my life, my own way, never giving Him thanks for any of it. How God must have been sorrowed over that! I was His beloved daughter and to make matters worse, I didn't feel the need to go to Jesus Christ as a mediator between God and I.

> *Then He said: "A certain man had two sons. And the younger of them said to his father, 'Father, give me the portion of goods that falls to me.' So he divided to them his livelihood. And not many days after, the younger son gathered all together, journeyed to a far country, and there wasted his possessions with prodigal living.*
> **- Luke 15:11-13**

My far country was represented by my moral and spiritual separation not actually moving, geographically. I was so egotistic that I actually felt that I could live my life, my way. Yes, I still talked to God, but I never gave Him a chance to be in a relationship with me. I might have thought that I was 'tight' with God, however, nothing was further from the truth.

God was such a loving Father, He gave His love to me extravagantly and freely and was always ready to be the Father that I never had and needed.

I was being a rebellious and wayward daughter and to make matters worse, I was wasting God's gifts to me. Everything I had was Gods and I had not been a good steward in particular with His money. It was His money that I spent on me, not giving Him a good return on His investment!

I was so ashamed at all of the opportunities that I had to advance His Kingdom with His money and didn't do!

Definitions of Prodigal

ADJECTIVE
1. **Spending money or resources freely and recklessly; wastefully extravagant.**
Synonyms: wasteful · extravagant · spendthrift · improvident · imprudent ·
2. **Having or giving something on a lavish scale.**
Synonyms: generous · lavish · liberal · unstinting · unsparing · bountiful · copious ·

NOUN
Prodigals (plural)
3. **A person who spends money in a recklessly extravagant way.**
Synonyms: profligate · prodigal · squanderer · waster · big spender · wastrel
https://www.thefreedictionary.com/prodigal

After reading the definitions of the word prodigal, I began to see where God could be described as being a prodigal Father with His gifts to each of us: **generous · lavish · liberal · unsparing · bountiful ·**

> *Then he went and joined himself to a citizen of that country, and he sent him into his fields to feed swine. And he would gladly have filled his stomach with the pods that the swine ate, and no one gave him anything.*
> **- Luke 15:15-16**

Being imprisoned is definitely hitting 'rock bottom.' In my rebellion, just like the lost son, I wondered what I was doing here. I knew all of the steps that had led me down to this point, going all of the way back to 2004. All of the poor choices that I had made and my separation from my Father and His Son, who loved me and was devoted to me.

> *"But when he came to himself, he said, 'How many of my father's hired servants have bread enough and to spare, and I*

perish with hunger! I will arise and go to my father, and will say to him, "Father, I have sinned against heaven and before you, and I am no longer worthy to be called your son. Make me like one of your hired servants."
- Luke 15:17-19

There had been times before being born-again that I wondered if God could ever forgive me for not acknowledging His son, Jesus Christ. I had never looked at it this way before, that in doing so, I was actually saying, you aren't God! After all, Jesus Christ is part of the Trinity. To deny any one of the Trinity is to deny them all. How could I have been so stupid, let alone, not caring anything about my eternal life!

I, like the lost son had to be humbled in order to 'get in my right mind.' And just like that son, I was so remorseful and knew that I had to beg for forgiveness. I needed to kneel before that cross and ask Jesus to forgive me for all of my sins and at the top of that list was in denying His divinity!

"And he arose and came to his father. But when he was still a great way off, his father saw him and had compassion, and ran and fell on his neck and kissed him. And the son said to him, 'Father, I have sinned against heaven and in your sight, and am no longer worthy to be called your son.'
- Luke 15:20-21

These are my favorite verses of this parable. The father is waiting, tirelessly waiting for the return of his son. He is spending all of his time anticipating the great return, it has become the focus of his life. In his joy, he 'fell on his neck and kissed him.' For the culture of that time, I have a feeling that this behavior would not have been expected, something the son had probably never dreamed would be his welcome back. I can feel the love and joy that the father was experiencing. As a mother, I understand what it feels like when I see the Crown Prince after a long absence.

"But the father said to his servants, 'Bring out the best robe and put it on him, and put a ring on his hand and sandals on his feet. And bring the fatted calf here and kill it, and let us eat

and be merry; for this my son was dead and is alive again; he was lost and is found.' And they began to be merry."
- Luke 22-24

Can you imagine that? The lost son was welcomed back, and given back the families ring which reinstated him as an important son in the family, an heir and would give him authority to transact family business. When his father gave him a pair of sandals, he was reinforcing the sons status as a family member, not that of a slave.

Can you imagine the Angels celebrating when I was adopted into the family of God? I can and it was glorious! Jesus clothed me in His Truth, His Light, His Joy, His Love and His PEACE!

From that day forward I was changed and I had been forgiven the worst possible sin, that of denying Jesus Christ as my Lord and Savior. Not only has it been forgiven, it has been forgotten! Praise God!

Praise to the LORD for His Love and Faithfulness

It is good to give thanks to the LORD, And to sing praises to Your name, O Most High;
- Psalm 92:1

Praise the LORD, all you Gentiles! Laud Him, all you peoples! For His merciful kindness is great toward us, And the truth of the LORD endures forever. Praise the LORD!
- Psalm 117:1-2

I will declare Your name to My brethren; In the midst of the assembly I will praise You. You who fear the LORD, praise Him! All you descendants of Jacob, glorify Him, And fear Him, all you offspring of Israel!

My praise shall be of You in the great assembly; I will pay My vows before those who fear Him. The poor shall eat and be

satisfied; Those who seek Him will praise the Lord*. Let your heart live forever!*
- **Psalm 23:22-23, 25-26**

The Happiness of Those Who Trust in God

I will bless the Lord *at all times; His praise shall continually be in my mouth. My soul shall make its boast in the* Lord*; The humble shall hear of it and be glad. Oh, magnify the* Lord *with me, And let us exalt His name together.*
- **Psalm 34:1-3**

CHAPTER 25

PEACE

Be anxious for nothing, but in everything by prayer and supplication, with thanksgiving, let your requests be made known to God; and the peace of God, which surpasses all understanding, will guard your hearts and minds through Christ Jesus.
- **Philippians 4:6-7**

Peace I leave with you, My peace I give to you; not as the world gives do I give to you. Let not your heart be troubled, neither let it be afraid.
- **John 14:27**

Grace be to you and peace from God the Father, and from our Lord Jesus Christ.
- **Galatians 1:3**

In his *Commentary on Galatians,* Martin Luther says that Paul chose those words carefully, and "that those two words [grace and peace] contain all that belongs to Christianity." He goes on further to say that "grace forgives sin, and peace makes the conscience quiet." Luther also adds that Paul's claim is that true peace can only come through grace. So dear readers, remember that in Christ, true peace is already within us, it is ours, through grace.

> **We are apt to think that everything that happens to us is to be turned into useful teaching; it is to be turned into something better than teaching, viz. into character. We shall find that the spheres God brings us into are not meant to teach us something but to make us something.**
> **– Oswald Chambers / <u>The Love of God</u>**

It had been a week since I last talked to the ARUM, so I waited in the day room so that I could again, sign up to see her. Finally it was my turn and when I entered her tiny office she asked me what I had come in for. Oh boy. I reminded her of my dilemma about paroling to Florida instead of Michigan. She looked through her notes and then proceeded to tell me that she had talked with my parole agent and he told her that I had to parole to Michigan because they had not started the Intra-state-transfer paperwork and there wasn't time to have it completed before my exit date.

I wasn't stunned, I wasn't even upset and I knew in that moment Jesus was there giving me His peace. After I was paroled, I figured out why the State didn't want to do my paperwork. If it is done while the inmate was still in prison, it is at no charge to the inmate, unlike when the paperwork is done once an inmate has been released with the fee being $300.00. As usual, money talks and confirms that inmates are a source of income to the state. Interesting enough when I paroled to Florida, my parole agent said that they didn't have a transfer fee….again, interesting.

I did have a contingency plan and that was to live with Jan until my intra- state-transfer was completed. So, I had to change the direction my mind was going and was amazed that anxiety hadn't overtaken me. Everything was different, I wasn't responding to events like I did before I was born-again, with each bump in the road I was actually feeling calmer and calmer. Jesus Christ, The Prince of Peace, was fighting my battles for me. That is just so awesome!

Just because I was in a state of serenity didn't mean that troubling things weren't happening all around me. One in particular was trying to get to me and I wasn't going to have it.

The water fountain in the kitchen area and in direct view for the C.O. was constantly being rigged to stay on continuously. This fountain had a cooling motor and I knew that it would break down with this kind of abuse. I had seen in happen in other units. The perpetrators would use the laundry ties and shove it in to make the water flow non-stop. So, every time I walked by, I removed it.

I eventually caught on to who was the major culprit and so, every time I saw her walk in the direction of the fountain, I would walk up and take the laundry tie out. I have to admit, it had become a game to me and I knew that it was really making this woman mad.

One day, she came up to me and stood almost nose to nose and asked why I kept doing that. I told her that it wasn't making the water any colder and was in fact hard on the motor. She said she didn't give a care what it was doing to the motor and that she was putting me on notice to stop it. I just laughed. I know that made her even madder, but I couldn't contain myself.

Of course, Father God, let me know what He thought about my tactics! That day the daily reading really hit home:

Be Steadfast

Therefore, beloved, looking forward to these things, be diligent to be found by Him in peace, without spot and blameless; - 2 Peter 3:14

I was spending more and more time in the library which was located in the kitchen area of the unit. It seemed like every day God was showing me books that he wanted me to see. That was the best variety of books I had seen in any of the units that I had been assigned to. I found out it was because when inmates go home, they don't want to take the books that they were given with them.

There were a lot of Bibles, AA books and a lot of Christian books. A few of them I read and actually took a few of them with me when I left. I was so grateful to God for finding me material that He wanted for me. By this time, I was all too aware that God was in charge and I was just following. It actually felt great to have someone leading me for a change.

I now know that comfort and peace can only be found through trusting God's plan for me. This has been a major shift in my thinking. I was always a planner, it was the only way I could feel safe, which in reality was just an illusion. The peace of the world is only temporary and the gift of Jesus Christ's peace is eternal. I am reminded of the 'trust game' where you stand in front of someone and have faith that they are going to catch you. I must confess that I have never been able to do it. I don't know if I could even do it today, I do know that I can and will trust in our Lord, I would stand in front of Him and just fall backwards, knowing, trusting that He would catch me.

I know that God delights in me and lavishes me with His favor, which results in my peace, I am referring to an overall feeling of well-being. "I am highly favored." The peace that I feel is like no other feeling and it is something I have never had before, what a gift!

> *And let the peace of God rule in your hearts, to which also you were called in one body; and be thankful.*
> **- Colossians 3:15**

> *The things which you learned and received and heard and saw in me, these do, and the God of peace will be with you.*
> **- Philippians 4:9**

> *When a man's ways please the LORD, He makes even his enemies to be at peace with him.*
> **- Proverbs 16:7**

> *Now may the God of hope fill you with all joy and peace in believing, that you may abound in hope by the power of the Holy Spirit.*
> **- Romans 15:13**

It was finally my day to be released. It happened early in the morning and I was the only one on that day to go. Many inmates stood at the threshold of their rooms to say good-bye. I was beaming, I couldn't help it, and it is a day I will always remember.

After leaving the unit, I had to go to the quartermaster for a new coat, new pants, blouse and new shoes. It was a cool crisp February day and I felt I was breathing fresh air, again, everything feeling new.

I had to walk clear across the campus to the gate on the west side. My box was heavy due to all of the books I was taking home, it was a good thing that I got to use a tray to move it.

I was motioned to have a seat when I arrived and waited only a few minutes before it was time to go through the 'bubble.' I had to be patted down, one last time, for what I didn't know. The bubble is two gates, once inside the gate behind you closes and the gate in front of you opens.

There were several people waiting in the reception area to see their inmate for a visit and they were all watching me. It was an overwhelming moment and there they were, the crown prince and his beautiful wife walking towards me. We embraced and I think I teared up, I really can't remember.

We walked outside of the doors and through the gate to FREEDOM!

> *Now may the God of peace Himself sanctify you completely; and may your whole spirit, soul, and body be preserved blameless at the coming of our Lord Jesus Christ.*
> **- 1 Thessalonians 5:23**

Thank you dear reader for taking this journey with me, from prison to peace. It has been a privilege to share my testimony of coming to Jesus Christ. Christ does promise a peace that will quiet your heart. Knowing that Jesus came into this world to heal my damaged relationship with God has brought peace to my troubled soul. Knowing that Jesus came to open wide the gates to heaven, bringing peace to my confused and sinful nature, I can live my best life.

The peace of Jesus, what a wonderful promise! Oftentimes, when I think of peace, I think about calmness, serenity, and stillness of heart. But the truth is, the peace which Jesus Christ gave to me is much more than just peace of mind. It's a peace (shalom) that surpasses human understanding. It represents wholeness, health, abundance, harmony, completion, perfection, contentment, and more.

It's a peace that has allowed me to sleep soundly in the midst of a darkened, sinful, fallen world, because I know that God is with me and that He will always guide me to safety.

It's a peace that has allowed me to walk boldly through the valley of the shadow of death, because I know that my Shepherd, Jesus Christ's rod will defend me from any danger, He is standing by, in case I fall to pick me up. It's a peace that has assured, soothed, healed, and redeemed me. I am REDEEMED!

It's a peace that was bought at a great price and yet it's always freely given. He who was sinless took all afflictions upon Himself, being the sacrifice for me so that I could receive the forgiveness, the gifts of the Spirit and His Peace.

When you don't have peace, you have a mind that is divided between legitimate worries and baseless destructive thoughts. The key to having unshakable peace is not to consider your current circumstances, but to keep your focus on God and His promises. I believe that when you have that peace, others around you can actually feel it surrounding you.

So what is your heart telling you today? Are you filled with peace and joy? Or are you filled with fear and worries?

Every time you choose peace, you're choosing to remain faithful and trust in God. Every time you choose fear, you're choosing to accept the devil's lies. Yes, it is a choice, a choice that's made according to what you pray about, what you believe, and what you confess to Jesus Christ.

So what will it be today? Will you accept the peace (shalom) that Jesus died for to give you?

> *If a man loves me, he will keep my word. My Father will love him, and we will come to him, and make our home with him. He who doesn't love me doesn't keep my words. The word which you hear isn't mine, but the Father's who sent me. I have said these things to you while still living with you. But the Counselor, the Holy Spirit, whom the Father will send in my name, will teach you all things, and will remind you of all that I said to you. Peace I leave with you.*
>
> *My peace I give to you; not as the world gives, I give to you. Don't let your heart be troubled, neither let it be fearful. You heard how I told you, 'I go away, and I come to you.' If you loved me, you would have rejoiced, because I said 'I am going to my Father;' for the Father is greater than I. Now I have told you before it happens so that when it happens, you may believe. I will no more speak much with you, for the prince of the world comes, and he has nothing in me. But that the world may know that I love the Father, and as the Father commanded me, even so I do. Arise, let's go from here.*
>
> **- John 14:23-31**

And the peace of God, which surpasses all understanding, will guard your hearts and minds through Christ Jesus.
- Philippians 4:7

But the wisdom that is from above is first pure, then peaceable, gentle, willing to yield, full of mercy and good fruits, without partiality and without hypocrisy.
- James 3:17

The Redemption at work in my actual life means the nature of God garrisoning me round; it *the God of peace* who sanctifies wholly; the security is almighty. The gift of the peace of Christ on the inside; the garrison of God on the outside, then I have to see that I allow the peace of God to regulate all that I do, that is where my responsibility comes in, "and let the peace of Christ rule," i.e., arbitrate, "in your hearts," and life will be full of praise at all times.
– Oswald Chambers / <u>The Highest Good</u>, page 113

Now may the Lord of peace Himself give you peace always in every way. The Lord be with you all.
– 2 Thessalonians 3:16

Printed in the United States
By Bookmasters